Determinants of Marketed Surplus in a Backward Economy

By the Same Author

– Genesis of Human Development in North East India: A Diagnostic Analysis
– Human Development: The New Approach to Development Strategies

---

About the Author

Keya Sengupta is presently a Professor at the Indian Institute of Management, Shillong and was formerly the Dean, School of Social Sciences and also the Head, Department of Economics at Assam Central University. Prof. Sengupta is engaged in teaching of Economics and Research for over thirty years. She has authored and also edited many books and published many research papers in journals of repute including *Artha Vijnana,* Man and Development, Finance India etc. She has also presented a good number of papers in national and international seminars and delivered lectures in many universities. Prof. Sengupta has also completed major Research Projects of UGC, ICSSR and UNDP and also undertaken Research Consultancy of CII and Planning Commission. Recently, she was selected for the Indo French Social Scientist Exchange Programme and was invited by Foundation Maison des Sciences de l' Hommes, Paris, France. She has also visited Belgium, Holland, Germany, Scotland and England in connection with various types of academic work.

Determinants of Marketed Surplus in a Backward Economy

A Case Study of Three Districts of South Assam

Keya Sengupta

CONCEPT PUBLISHING COMPANY PVT. LTD., NEW DELHI-110059

ISBN-978-81-8069-696-1

First Published 2010

Published and Printed by

Concept Publishing Company Pvt. Ltd.
Regd. Office:
A/15-16, Commercial Block, Mohan Garden
New Delhi-110059 (India)
Phones : 25351460, 25351794, *Fax* : 091-11-25357109
Email : publishing@conceptpub.com,
Website: www.conceptpub.com

Editorial Office:
H-13, Bali Nagar, New Delhi-110 015, India.

Cataloging in Publication Data--*Courtesy:* D.K. Agencies (P) Ltd. <docinfo@dkagencies.com>

Sengupta, Keya, 1957-
Determinants of marketed surplus in a backward economy : a case study of three districts of south Assam / Keya Sengupta.
p. cm.
Includes bibliographical references (p.) and index.
ISBN 9788180696961

1. Surplus agricultural commodities--India--Barak Valley. 2. Farm produce--India--Barak Valley--Marketing. I. Title.

DDC 338.170954162 22

Dedicated to

My Parents

Preface

Studies relating to the generation of marketable and marketed surplus has tremendous significance for agriculturally dominated backward regions. Generation of a satisfactory quantum of marketed surplus can increase capital formation, real saving and real investment. It can boost agro based industries and thus raise the welfare of the people and the overall prosperity of the region. This in turn can prevent unwanted and unplanned migration from rural areas to urban areas. Generation of adequate quantum of marketed surplus can have a strong backward as well as forward linkages with the rest of the economy, so that creating a strong agricultural base through marketed surplus can be used as an instrument to build up the entire economy.

It is in this context that the present study assumes crucial significance, because there is hardly any work relating to this crucial area of marketed surplus that has been undertaken for South Assam, inspite of the fact that the region is dominated both in terms of employment as well as in terms of the contribution to NSDP by the agricultural sector. The present work therefore attempts to make a modest but significant contribution towards fulfilling this vital gap, which is expected to go a long way in helping not only empirical research but also for policy purposes.

The entire work is divided into six chapters along with numerous sub-sections. The first chapter introduces the subject and discusses the significance of the study of marketed surplus for a less developed region as well as for India and particularly for South Assam. The second chapter gives a broad outline of the various studies on marketed surplus that has been undertaken in India. It also focuses attention to the scenario of agricultural marketing in India. The third chapter gives the socio-economic background and also highlights the existing agricultural practices and cropping pattern of the study area. The chapter also deals with the objectives and the methodology of the study and focuses attention to the conceptual framework of the study. In the fourth chapter we have analysed the primary data and attempted to identify the significant determinants of marketed surplus in South Assam. The fifth chapter deals exclusively with the empirical testing of the models that has been developed for the purpose of the study, and makes a detailed study of the estimated results and comes out with the main findings of the study. The sixth chapter deals with the main findings and conclusions of the study.

It is expected that the book will be of immense help for not only researchers but also post graduate students in general and particularly students of the north-eastern region, since this is one of the first book of its kind pertaining to this region.

Keya Sengupta

Acknowledgements

I am thankful to all those who have helped me in the collection of primary data, which has formed the very base of the study. Data had to be collected from various remote areas of southern Assam under very difficult conditions, since most areas are afflicted by regular floods and other calamities of weather. I am also thankful to the library facilities offered to me by the Indian Institute of Advanced Studies, Shimla Giri Institute of Development Studies, Lucknow, JNU, New Delhi, Indian Institute of Public Administration, New Delhi, Indian Council of Social Science Research, New Delhi, and Assam University.

I am also thankful to my typist for completing the work in an extremely proficient manner. My thanks are also due to all those who have helped me directly as well as indirectly in completing the work.

Keya Sengupta

Contents

1

Marketed Surplus: Role and Importance

1.1 Introduction

Studies relating to the agricultural sector have always put greater emphasis on production rather than on marketing of the agricultural produce that is generated. Issues relating to the generation of surplus from the production of agricultural products and selling them in the market has always received a secondary place, in most research work. Agricultural production and marketability of the produce are however two sides of the same coin, and one is incomplete without the other. Generation of adequate quantum of agricultural surplus to be sold in the market, is an essential and integral part of, not only agricultural development in particular, but of the overall strategy of economic development of a nation/region. Such studies assume crucial significance for less developing or totally agriculturally dominated areas. The development of such economies is governed totally by the prosperity of the agricultural sector. The prosperity of the agricultural sector in turn depends not only on the quantity of agricultural produce, but more importantly on marketability of the agricultural produce.

In the agricultural marketing scenario, it is to be noted that the entire production of agricultural produce, is not offered for sale in the market. The farmers retain a considerable portion of the produce for self consumption, seeds and inventories for the next season, payments in kind to either the labourers or creditors and normal wastage that occurs during the course of handling transportation and sale of the produce. The total production minus these amounts gives rise to marketable surplus, which may either be zero, negative or positive, depending upon the total production of agricultural produce, size of the farms and the relative weight of the above mentioned factors. The entire amount offered for sale in the market or the marketable surplus as it is referred to, may not be sold off totally. The amount of the total quantum generated for sale that is actually sold in the market, is termed as *marketed surplus*. Factors which determine the quantum of marketed surplus are different from the factors which govern marketable surplus. The latter which is the main focus of our study depends on factors like the prevailing price in the market, cash need of the farmers, holding capacity, transport storage facilities etc.

Both marketable and marketed surplus have tremendous potential for ensuring prosperity in the agricultural sector because efficient marketing of the surplus that has been generated, can boost up capital formation and real saving and real investment in the agricultural sector. Rise in real income in an inflation-free agriculturally dominated economy through increase in real agricultural surplus can raise welfare of the nation as a whole. Welfare can also be raised through establishment of rural industries which are often agro-based. Such industries are totally dependent on the generation of surpluses in the agricultural sector. Rise in real income in the agricultural sector, not merely through higher production, but by generation of higher surplus for sale which increases the demand for products of the secondary and tertiary sectors. Through the operation of the multiplier effect this enlarges the scope for the expansion of the economy. Higher potential of investment opportunities and employment generation through various phases are the direct benefit which the entire economy can expect from such prosperity of the agricultural sector.

It also needs to be mentioned here that marketed surplus if satisfactory can arrest unproductive migration from rural to the urban sectors, who migrate in search of better economic opportunities and petty jobs in towns and cities. Consequently, numerous problems associated with slum condition of living may be reduced.

As far as the Indian economy is concerned, the policy-makers are caught in the web of subsidy syndrome to the agricultural sector. Poverty of the farmers is cited as the most plausible argument for continuation of subsidy. Any withdrawal of subsidy is expected to have disastrous consequences on the agricultural sector, according to the supporters of subsidy. At the same time, growing subsidy means a huge drain of scarce resources, which could have been more profitably used in other much more finance starved sectors of the economy. Prosperity of the agricultural sector through adequate generation of marketed surplus by raising real income of the farmers may also reduce the pressure of much debated issue of subsidy to the agricultural sector and can go a long way in giving relief to a capital starved sector in particular and the economy in general.

It is therefore evident that marketable and marketed surplus is the source of not only agricultural development but also overall economic development. Such surpluses converted into cash can serve as the correct strategy for long-term economic development.

1.2 Marketed Surplus in the Context of the Indian Economy

Marketed surplus has played a very significant role in shaping the broad contours of development of the various states of the Indian economy. Higher yields witnessed in the post Green Revolutionera in different states of the country has resulted in levels of economic development, which have not been uniform in any of the states. This is mainly due to the fact that it is the marketed surplus and not the actual quantum of production alone, which determines the real prosperity of the state. Such experience reveals that both agricultural production and marketed surplus should receive simultaneous attention by policy-makers. States of Punjab followed by Haryana have consistently recorded extremely high levels of marketed surplus, which has resulted in expediting levels of economic development. Some of the other States like Gujarat, Tamil Nadu and Andhra Pradesh have followed a similar pattern of growth which can be traced to the generation of satisfactory quantity of marketed surplus. In contrast, the states of Orissa, Assam, Bihar which have witnessed a low quantum of marketed surplus, have not only suffered from a low level of economic development but have also revealed problems of unproductive migration, lack of rural industrialization and a backward agrarian base.

In states which are relatively backward, an increase in agricultural production does not give rise to marketed surplus immediately. Higher production results in higher consumption by the farmers themselves, the pent up demand of the poor farmers unsatisfied for years, due to poverty, tends to be satisfied initially, when agricultural production rises. Consequently, rise in self-consumption by the farmers, prevents rise of marketed surplus. In regions dominated by small and marginal farmers, where agriculture is carried on at a subsistence level, higher production therefore only results in higher consumption, instead of raising directly the quantity offered for sale. The north-eastern region of India too, where till recently not much effort was made to raise agricultural production is conspicuous by the absence of large sized farms and big farmers. Farmers who are mostly small and marginal are caught up in a vicious circle of poverty. Consequently, they have a high propensity to consume, and a slightly higher income and higher production results in satisfying their pent up demand, thereby absorbing a significant proportion of the increased production, in satisfying consumption needs, instead of raising marketable surplus immediately.

Studies have revealed that once the farmers attain the optimum level of consumption, beyond which they are unable to increase their level of consumption, higher production in the agricultural sector may be channelised into the market for sale. It is for this reason that generation of marketed surplus is not directly proportional to the rise in agricultural production.

Marketed surplus has therefore both a backward as well as forward linkage with economic prosperity of the farmers. Just as farmers who are well-off can afford to offer a higher volume as marketed surplus, a higher quantum of marketed surplus also in turn can raise the economic condition of the farmers. The rise in the standard of living encourages capital formation in the agricultural sector, which is an urgent necessity for this capital starved sector, particularly where capital investments are extremely crucial. Capital formation in turn encourages better and modern techniques of production. Use of modern inputs, HYV (High Yielding Variety), irrigational and other facilities can be availed of by such prosperous farmers, which in turn will further raise production in this sector, leading to higher marketed surplus.

Besides raising the prosperity of the agricultural sector itself, marketed surplus can also help to raise the capital formation of the non-agricultural sector as well. Rise in the income of the farmers, due to a rise in marketed surplus raises the demand for all types of products, including the products of the industrial sector. Increase in the demand for industrial items by a significant proportion of the rural population will encourage further investment, profitability and capital formation in the industrial sector. Increased income in the agricultural sector has numerous other beneficial effects as mentioned earlier, such as an increase in rural savings. Such savings can be siphoned back not only to the agricultural sector, but can be used for the overall economic development of the nation or the region as a whole.

The problem of unemployment in the rural sector may be solved by the establishment of agro-based industries, which may be dependent on the generation of marketed surplus in the rural areas. Absorption of rural manpower by such industries by relieving the agricultural sector from the burden of underemployment, not only raises the productivity of land per capita but may also arrest constant migration from rural to urban sectors. Numerous problems associated with rural as well as urban development may thus be simultaneously taken care of through the generation of adequate quantum of marketed surplus.

1.3 Marketed Surplus and Socio-economic Development

Higher living standards of the farmers can also benefit the agricultural sector, and raise marketed surplus, in yet another manner which many researchers dealing with marketed surplus have often overlooked. Higher income, not only means a higher standard of living, but it also results in a significant improvement, in the socio-economic condition of the farmers. Realisation will dawn among such farmers, with a relatively high living standard, regarding the necessity and importance of education in general and also extension education in particular. A serious ailment characterizing our agricultural sector, is the mass of illiterate farmers, who are neither aware of the various ways of increasing production or getting remunerative prices for marketed surplus. A rise in the living standard of the farmers may ensure a minimum level of education. An educated farmer is better equipped than an uneducated farmer, regarding the availability of institutional credit rather than allow himself to be exploited by the village money-lenders. He is also more knowledgeable regarding the best techniques of production and is more conscious of the optimum use of agricultural inputs and other resources at his disposal. He is more informed, relating to the market price of the product he is offering for sale, and is less liable to be exploited in weights and measures and in paying unwarranted commission to the various agencies. He is thereby more motivated to get remunerative market prices for his product, which provides incentives in raising not only agricultural production, but also in increasing the quantum of marketed surplus as well, since higher margin will be his motivating and main driving force. This will directly result in raising the level of rural savings and capital formation in the capital starved agricultural sector of the economy.

For any country with a huge population the pivotal role of marketed surplus need not be over emphasized. It is the generation of adequate quantity of marketed surplus, which can feed her teeming millions. Absence of marketed surplus would compel the nation to import foodgrains, a disturbing feature which had characterized the Indian economy prior to the mid-sixties. Valuable foreign exchange, so, essential for the development of a nation, is wasted in the process. Consequently, development efforts are slackened. Coupled with the wastage of valuable foreign exchange, shortage of domestic availability of agricultural products due to inadequate supply of marketed surplus may raise prices of foodgrains, in the face of perennial shortage in supply and constant increase in demand. The internal as well as the external balance of the nation will thereby be in jeopardy.

A long-term benefit of improved socio-economic condition would also result in reducing the growth rate of population in the rural sector, since studies have revealed that population growth has a negative correlationship with higher standard of living. This trend may therefore go a long way in releasing the pressure of population on land, which is another problem characterizing the Indian agricultural sector. This results in not only raising labour productivity in the agricultural sector, decline in the burden of underemployment but a rise in marketed surplus as well. Reduced population pressure also means lower level of consumption by the farmers themselves, and lower consumption implies higher marketable surplus, since evidences suggest a negative correlationship between consumption by the farmers and marketed surplus.

Experience in the Indian economy reveal that a rise in the price of foodgrains raises the general price level, since the Indian economy is based on "foodgrain standards" unlike "wage standards" of developed nations (Sengupta, 1997). Any unwarranted behaviour of marketable surplus, especially in the Indian context, can be wrought with dangerous consequences for the economy as a whole with such price sensitivity. One therefore, cannot agree more with the opinion of W.H. Nichollas who maintains that, until the underdeveloped countries succeed in achieving and sustaining a reliable food surplus, they have not fulfilled the fundamental preconditions for economic development (Nichollas, 1963).

1.4 Necessity of the Study in the Context of Barak Valley of South Assam

The uneven development of the agricultural sector between time and space in different regions of India, is a peculiar feature, characterizing Indian agriculture, necessitating wide diversifications in policy variations, not only between regions, but even within a region itself. The north-eastern region of India, which has historically witnessed a relative isolation, presents more diversity in comparison to the rest of the country, in terms of its social, cultural and economic context of growth. Even within the region itself, broad distinctive features of differences are clearly visible. It is therefore, essential that any developmental effort, attempted for the region, be it in agricultural, or industrial sector, if viewed in a uniform context of the overall developmental efforts of the country, may only invite frustrations and consequent failures. As a result, the north-eastern economy is in great danger of being polarized, which no serious policy-maker can afford to ignore. It is in this light, that the selection of the plain region of South Assam consisting of three districts of Cachar, Karimganj and Hailakandhi, known as Barak Valley assumes importance, for the purpose of the present study. Although a part of Assam, the Valley has some distinctive, locational, economic, sociological features of its own, which calls for a special investigation of its problem, with the objective of helping the policy-makers for long-term growth and development.

The dominance of the agricultural sector is a feature, characterizing the economy of the north-eastern region and more so of Barak Valley of South Assam. It is this sector of the economy which can ultimately define the broad contours of growth for the region as a whole. Providing a strong foundation to the overall development efforts of the valley is the responsibility of the agricultural sector, both in terms of its productivity as well as marketability.

The role of marketed surplus in the agriculturally dominated but backward economy has prompted us to undertake the present work. Though numerous studies on various aspects of the agricultural sector, as well as marketed surplus have been conducted for the agriculturally advanced regions of the country, the difference in the agro-climatic and socio-economic conditions reduces the scope of the applicability of such studies in our case. Pivotal role of marketable surplus notwithstanding, no attempt has so far been made to analyse the movement of marketable or marketed surplus or their determinants. The study assumes added importance for this valley with its constituent units of Cachar, Karimganj and Hailakandi districts, all of which taken together, occupies only 9 per cent of the geographical area of the state, and bear 13 per cent of its population. Density of population in the valley is thus one of the highest in the north-eastern region, resulting in acute unemployment problem as well as overcrowding problem in the agricultural sector, giving rise to the problem of underemployment. The geographical isolation of the valley, dampens any major entrepreneurial effort both public and private, for setting up any industrial venture with little possibility of any kind of change in the economic scenario in the near future. The Barak Valley is therefore marked by high incidence of poverty, with majority of the farmers who are small and marginal, practicing traditional forms of cultivation. Any development of the valley warrants a strong agricultural base, as a first step towards long-term economic growth, which calls for a serious investigation and research into the present form, pattern and nature of performance of the sector.

Added to the usual features characterizing a backward and traditional agricultural sector of the valley, marketing of the agricultural produce, assumes additional challenge for the valley.

1.5 Agricultural Marketing Scenario in India

The agricultural marketing system in India is generally marked by an exploitative and inefficient nature of operation. Chain of intermediaries, enhance the complexity of agricultural marketing in India. Such intermediaries in the process of acquiring the marketable surplus from farmers scattered all over the region only explore the various possibilities of adding to the price of the product through various forms of commissions and charges merely by a change in the time, place and value of the products offered for sale (ICSSR). Emergence of Government agencies as direct purchasers from the farmers, though has gained considerable momentum in recent years, the benefit of such government purchases has remained confined mostly to a few regions. It is still a common experience, that in regions dominated by poor farmers, significant proportion of the marketed surplus is purchased by the commission agents, who are the intermediaries between the producers and the wholesalers. The result is that the benefits of a constant rise in procurement prices, have either gone to the intermediaries or the rich farmers, with the economic condition of the poor farmers, remaining the same as ever.

A highly disturbing feature of agricultural marketing, particularly from the point of view of income distribution in the rural sector, is the considerable fluctuation in the price level at which marketed surplus is purchased from the producers. Small and marginal farmers, who lack storage facilities and who are in immediate need of cash are compelled to sell their produce in the post harvest season at a much lower price, whereas the produce of rich farmers can be stored and released during the lean seasons, when prices are much higher. This results in increasing the hardships of not only the poor farmers, but the ultimate consumers as well, increasing most often the unwarranted margins of the middlemen and the traders. Prevalence of this tendency has also prevented stability of agricultural prices, and frequent fluctuations of agricultural prices in turn, affects adversely the general price level, since in the Indian economy, general prices depend upon agricultural prices as revealed by various studies relating to the Indian economy.

A serious constraint to agricultural marketing and thus market arrivals of agricultural produce, in various markets, is the lack of transportation facilities. Most of the remote villages of the country are unconnected by fair weather roads or are too far away from the nearest markets. Inaccessibility of the villages, compels the farmers to offer their produce, almost at a throw away price, rather than transport their produce at high costs to the markets or carry the produce themselves on foot and travel a few miles for reaching the nearest markets. Inadequacy of any serious arrivals of agricultural produce from remote villages is a very difficult proposition. The problem is further compounded during the monsoons, when these villages are totally cut off from the nearest markets for months together. Consequently, such a situation provides scope to the unscrupulous traders and middleman to take further advantage of such infrastructual constraints and exploit the poor farmers, since they have no other avenues to dispose off their produce, but to sell at a throwaway price to these intermediaries.

Economic condition of the farmers is a reflection of the smooth flow of their produce to the markets in adequate quantity. Dominance of small and marginal farmers in India, with fragmented and small holdings has not only brought down the productivity of land, but has also made proper estimation of market arrivals highly uncertain and unpredictable. Big farmers have the ability to hold back supply and release them during lean seasons, and can afford to wait for a favourable time when prices are more remunerative. Strong economic condition, of which size of land holding is an important criterion, do not necessitate the immediate sale of their produce, since requirement of immediate cash from the sale of their produce is not the main concern of rich farmers. Evidence drawn from the Indian economic scenario, therefore suggests that marketed surplus to a large extent is determined by the economic condition of the farmers, not only due to their higher level of production, but also due to their stronger economic position which can considerably influence the determination of market arrivals. It is revealed that erratic behaviour of market arrivals, is a characteristic feature of regions dominated by poor farmers, whereas reverse is the case with regions having farmers with strong economic position.

1.6 Agricultural Marketing Scenario in the North Eastern Region

It is therefore pertinent to take stock of the agricultural marketing scenario of the North-Eastern region, against the background of agricultural marketing for the country as a whole. North-Eastern region, is a predominantly agricultural region, where a major percentage of the population are engaged directly or indirectly in this sector, where cultivation of food crops rather than the cultivation of cash crops receive greater importance. Notwithstanding this, the region is marked by one of the lowest level of agricultural production in the country, with a significant gap between demand and supply necessitating bringing of foodgrains from the other regions of the country.

Geographical isolation of the region coupled with heavy monsoons and occurrence of regular floods are some of the special problems of the region, which severely compels any serious attempt at regularizing market arrivals of the farmers produce. Hills which occupy 70 per cent of its total geographical area, with numerous hilly and turbulent rivers, act as serious bottlenecks for the construction of roads, which form the nervous system for the smooth flow of market arrivals of foodgrains. Even the construction of railway system, which form the chief means of transporting the produce to the main marketing center in the other parts of the country, is a difficult proposition in this hilly terrain. The few roads that are existing at present are also inaccessible during the major part of the year, due to heavy monsoons and frequent landslides and floods, since a major portion of the roads of the region is unsurfaced. It is worth highlighting at this juncture that the percentage of surfaced road to total road length in the North-Eastern Region is only 27.08 per cent, and in Assam, it is merely 15.73 per cent as against the all-India figure of 50.52 per cent. This is inspite of the fact that roads are the main source of transport and communication in the region.

The region is also marked by the absence of any regulated markets worth mentioning, compared to all-India situation. Inadequate markets coupled with transportation problems encourages exploitation of small farmers by money-lenders and middlemen. Money-lenders in lieu of the money loaned out by them often take away the entire produce of the farmers or they are left to be purchased by the middlemen at a throwaway price leaving the farmers with no option, but to sell their produce at whatever price is offered to them. The village farmers sometimes carry their produce on their heads to the nearest rural market, walking for long distance, just to sell a small portion of their produce. The little money which they get are spent by these poor farmers, to purchase non-agricultural goods, at a much higher price. All these features not only contribute in reducing the quantum of marketed surplus, but also discourages them from increasing this quantum in the future. Motivation to increase marketed surplus is further damped, by exploitation of the farmers, on account of undue commissions, and unfair weights and measures, heavy indebtedness, lack of storage facilities and the awareness that any attempt to increase marketed surplus in the future means higher profit for the middlemen and the traders, rather than to the poor farmers themselves.

1.7 Generation of Marketable Surplus and Economic Development of Backward Regions

The pivotal role of economic development is to achieve self-sufficiency in every aspect of its economy. Particularly during the era of economic liberalization and globalisation with its emphasis on industrialization and service sector, a strong agricultural base is indispensable. Generation of adequate quantum of agricultural surplus, particularly of staple food like paddy or wheat is absolutely essential for feeding the manpower of the industrial and service sector. In the absence of such smooth coordination between the various sectors, attempts at expansion of the economy of a less developed nation may be totally stunted. For such economies, efficient system of marketing has both forward as well as backward linkages with the rest of the economy. Therefore developing a strong marketing base for disposal of marketed surplus, is not only essential for the agricultural sector alone, but is extremely important for the entire economy.

Farmers are encouraged to produce not only for their consumption, but also to dispose off as surplus, only when they gets a remunerative price for their products. Such prices can be ensured only when the economy is sufficiently sound in all other aspects, and when a major share of the price is not appropriated by various middlemen or the numerous channels of marketing. When all such measures are ensured, farmers are encouraged to go in for capital formation, without the desire for which no programme of generating surplus can be successful. Therefore surplus needs to be sold at prices sufficiently high, not only to meet their cost of production, but to enable them to have enough margin, so that capital formation in agriculture can be encouraged and even in backward areas, farmers are encouraged to go in for adoption of new technologies in agriculture. Generation of marketable surplus is therefore encouraged through development of a efficient marketing system.

The significance of marketable and marketed surplus in forging a link between producers and consumers, particularly for an agrarian economy, need not be overemphasized. Though studies relating to marketed surplus during economic liberalization and globalisation are often pushed to the backstage, yet inadequate generation of marketed surplus, may compel the nation to spend valuable foreign exchange for importing foodgrains. During such periods, increased income from various sectors of the economy raises demand for foodgrains. Consequently, the agrarian sector should not only be totally self-dependent, but should also provide a strong support base for the rest of the economy. Generation of marketed surplus during such times is therefore extremely crucial. Surplus also plays a crucial role for providing raw materials to the industrial sector, which paves the way for the success of globalisation.

Rural savings, which are so essential for the purpose of building up a strong rural base, during economic transition can be brought about only through marketed surplus. Sufficient quantum of marketed surplus results in raising income of the farmers which in turn increases rural savings. Rural base of the economy can also be strengthened through marketed surplus by encouraging agro-based industries. Such industries, which are totally based on raw products of various nature, directly from the agricultural sector are often localized in the rural sector itself. Such efforts if successful can also provide employment opportunities to the growing population of the agricultural sector and relieve the agricultural sector from the problem of underemployment which actually lowers productivity in the agricultural sector. Such efforts in turn may only raise productivity in the agricultural sector which may again help in increasing marketable surplus. It is therefore pertinent that, marketed surplus and economic development is highly interrelated and any nation which desires to speed up its economic development on a long-term sustainable basis has to give due importance to the generation of marketed surplus.

Generation of surplus is not only essential for meeting rising domestic demand, but if given a proper boost may help the nation to earn foreign exchange through its exports. Such an effort can prove to be more significant for a backward country or an agriculturally dominated nation rather than totally industrialized one. If a nation during the era of globalisation has to divert her foreign resources for importing foodgrains to meet her domestic demand, she will certainly fall back in global competition. Such crisis can be successfully tided over through generation of marketed surplus. Food self-sufficiency and food security are the essential pre-conditions for a nation to launch its programme of economic development. Therefore generation of marketed surplus is an integral part of any programme of economic development.

India had been a net importer of foodgrains till late sixties, when she was heavily dependent on other countries for import of foodgrains. This resulted in heavy drain of its foreign exchange resources, due to which the economic development had received a set back. Backward nature of Indian agriculture had resulted in generation of extremely insignificant quantum of marketed surplus. As a result, share of imports in the net availability of cereals was 16 per cent during 1966. With the advent of Green Revolution and improved marketing facilities, volume of marketed surplus too witnessed a sizeable increase, so that from early eighties, net share of imports to internal consumption of foodgrains have become almost negligible.

Price mechanism plays a pivotal role in determining the behaviourial pattern of the economic forces of demand and supply in the economy. In an economy dominated by the agrarian sector, prices of agricultural products have a crucial role to play in determining the general pattern of prices in the economy. Stability of prices in the agricultural sector, in turn can be ensured only through regular generation of marketed surplus. Frequent price fluctuations due to irregularity of market arrivals during post-harvest season or lean season, serves as a disincentive to the farm sector, particularly the small and marginal farmers. The inter-season and inter-year price fluctuations can be avoided by building sufficient quantum of buffer stocks, for the purpose of which steady flow of marketed surplus has to be ensured.

Marketable surplus has played a very important role in the economic development of countries like Russia, China and Japan. Each of these nations had taken special measures to augment marketed surplus in their respective countries, with the special objective of speeding up their rate of economic growth through resource transfer from agricultural sector to the industrial sector. Realising the importance of marketable surplus for initiating the process of long-term development, most of these nations laid emphasis on augmenting their agricultural produce, which was followed by a deliberate policy to augmenting marketed surplus which was subsequently used for the purpose of economic development. China for instance, increased her marketed surplus by organization of agrarian cooperatives. Collection of agricultural taxes in kind, facilitated flow of goods between agricultural and industrial sector by supplying consumer goods to peasants, provision of easy credit to farmers and guarantee of remunerative prices to the farmers. On the other hand, Soviet Russia emphasized the strategy of compulsory grain collection from collective farms, as a means of mopping up marketable surplus. Therefore ensuring a steady flow of marketable surplus for the purpose of long-term economic development has for long being a part of policy-measures, particularly for agrarian economies.

The rural base of the economy can also be strengthened through marketed surplus, by encouraging agro-based industries. Such industries which are totally based on raw products of various nature directly from the agricultural sector are often localized in the rural sector itself. Such efforts if successful can also provide employment opportunities to the growing population of the agricultural sector, and relieve the agricultural sector from the problem of underdevelopment, which actually lowers productivity of agriculture. Such efforts in turn may only raise productivity in the agricultural sector, which may again help in increasing marketed surplus. It is therefore pertinent that marketed surplus and economic development is highly interrelated, and any nation which desires to speed up its economic development on a long-term sustainable basis has to give due importance to the generation of marketed surplus.

References

Chakrabarty, Rajendra Mohon (1986): "Marketable Surplus of Foodgrains in Developing Economy" *Arthaniti*, Vol. II.

Dubey, V. (1963) "The Marketed Agricultural Surplus and Economic Growth in Underdeveloped Countries" *Economic Journal*, Vol. 73.

Jain, S.C. (Ed.) P. (1967): "Problems of Agricultural Development in India" Kitab Mahal, Allahabad.

Kahlon, A.S. (1961): "Problems of Marketable Surplus in Indian Agriculture" *Indian Journal of Agricultural Economies*, Vol. 16.

Mathon P.K. (1970): "Role of Marketable Food Surplus in Economic Development" *Asian Economic Review*, Vol. 12.

Mathur, P.N. (1961): "Marketable Surplus Function of Food and Price Fluctuations in a Developing Economy" *Kyklos*, Vol. 14.

Nichollas, W.H. (1963): "An Agricultural Surplus as a Factor in Economic Development" *Journal of Political Economy*, Vol. 7.

Prasad, A. and J. Prasad (1994) "Development Planning for Agriculture" Mittal Publication, New Delhi.

Prasad, S. (1985): "*Agricultural Marketing in India*" Mittal Publication, New Delhi.

Sengupta, K. (1997): "Genesis of Inflation in India: A Diagnostic Analysis" *Finance India*, Vol. XI, New Delhi.

2

Pattern and Nature of Marketable and Marketed Surplus and Agricultural Marketing in India

2.1 Introduction

Numerous studies on marketable and marketed surplus have been undertaken in India, examining various aspects of agricultural produce coming to the market. Analysis of some of the relevant work on the subject will enable us to get an overall perspective of the trend and the behaviourial pattern of this crucial area of agricultural sector. Such behaviourial trend will reveal the regional characteristics of marketed surplus, which will enable us to view the performance of Barak Valley *vis-a-vis* that of the other regions. It would also highlight the areas that may require greater attention by way of research and policy prescription in Barak Valley, as far as generation of marketable surplus, particularly paddy, is concerned. The analysis will therefore focus attention on all types of work on marketable surplus where surplus will be examined with respect to size group of land holdings, income groups, prices, productivity and other variables. The study will further examine the work, where surplus will be estimated both with the help of direct as well as indirect methods. It is an empirical reality that various factors such as productivity, cropping pattern, change in marketing strategy and market structure have been affecting agricultural surplus over time. Consequently, we feel that it is more pertinent to examine the surplus over time, rather than segregate the work according to the nature of the study. The analysis will therefore concentrate on decade-wise examination of the work done on marketable surplus.

2.2 Trend of Marketable Surplus in India

One of the pioneering works undertaken in this respect in India, was by Dharm Narain for national level data for all agricultural produce relating to the year 1950-51. Data for the purpose had been obtained from National Income Accounts Farm Management Surveys, All-India Rural Credit Surveys of RBI and NSS data. The work was related to the distribution of marketed surplus of farm produce by big groups. One of the pivotal findings of this work was that marketed surplus as a proportion of output in the country as a whole followed a U-shaped pattern in relation to the size of land holdings. The ratio of surplus declines as the size of holding increases till 10-15 acres of land holding and steadily increases thereafter. The study also revealed that holdings below 15 acres contributed more than one half and those below 10 acres, nearly one half of the total marketable surplus. The study further revealed that marketed surplus had a negative response to a rise in price. The possible reason could be that for the small farmers fixed cash requirement does not compel him to increase sale, particularly the distress sale. Consequently, higher prices encourages him to cut down on sales and increase his own consumption.

Another significant work conducted during the fifties was by Prof. Dandekar, entitled, "Prices, Production and Marketed Surplus of Foodgrains". In this work, it was revealed that large farmers with land-holdings of 30 acres and above, who represent 24 per cent of the total farmers, control over 60 per cent of the area under foodgrains and account for 80 per cent of marketed surplus, particularly that of jowar. In contrast, farmers with less than 5 acres of land, who accounted for 25 per cent of total number of farmers, had no marketable surplus, but had large sales.

J.P. Bhattacharjee in his work conducted during the same period entitled "Changing Characteristics of the Flow of Foodgrains Supplies from Farmers", for the states of Bihar, Orissa and West Bengal studied the behaviourial pattern of marketed surplus, with respect to the development of the village. The study revealed that marketed surplus in relation to output in most backward villages was lower even from large-sized holdings, because disposals in kind was much higher in comparison to developed villages. In the latter type of villages, marketed surplus of large-sized farms appeared to increase sharply. In a decade-wise comparative analysis, the author focused attention to the fact that, during the early forties and fifties, there was a sharp increase in the relative marketed surplus of large farmers followed by a decrease by small and medium sized farmers, to the extent of 25 per cent and 16 per cent respectively. A decrease in the level of distress sale coupled with the rise in precautionary and speculative motives in influencing marketed surplus, are some of the other significant findings of Bhattacharjee's study.

Another significant work undertaken with data for the period of fifties and early sixties was by Raj Krishna entitled, "Marketed Surplus Function for a Subsistence Crop—An analysis with Indian data" for the country as a whole. The work is based on a wide range of samples collected for households for a poor and partially monetized economy. Findings relate to the relationship between marketed surplus and total output, and not with the relationship with size holdings. The study revealed that marketed surplus displayed a linear trend, in a majority of cases, analysed with a negative intercept. Non-linear relationship was revealed in case of very poor and very rich farmers. Positive relationship between output and marketed surplus was found even in case of small output. Apart from output of subsistence crops, income was the second best predictor of marketed surplus. However, unlike most other studies, size of land-holdings appeared to be the worst predictor of marketable surplus. The study could not throw much light on price elasticity of marketed surplus, due to the existence of non-monetised peasant economy, from where the data was collected. However, the work could not throw light on output elasticity of marketed surplus.

The other work that is extremely important in the context of marketed surplus is that of Utsa Patnaik's (1975), work with national level data for the period 1960-61. Her findings reveal that marketed surplus increased in a linear fashion in response to output, unlike the 'U' pattern as maintained by Narain. The study also revealed that medium and big farmers contribute a larger proportion of marketed surplus to output whereas the proportion of smaller farmers decline over time. Factors responsible for this are the tendency for higher concentration of resources among the former category of farmers and the reverse in case of the latter. Findings of her work reveal that no size class records negative marketed surplus. The reason as the author herself contends is that the estimated quantity of marketed surplus does not include the quantity that is repurchased by the farmers. Besides, she has also used gross value of output of agriculture deducting the estimated retentions from this. The output thus estimated includes the non-food crops as well as the value of the produce from plantations, such as tea, coffee, rubber, coconut, arecanut and others. Inclusion of such items may not give us the true picture of marketed surplus, since such products are operated under highly commercialized and big holding conditions. Consequently, behaviourial pattern of small and marginal farmers, who dominate Indian agricultural scene, particularly with respect to paddy cannot be reflected in any manner.

Even for studies relating to some South Indian villages, conducted by Partha Sarathy and Subba Rao, "Production and Marketed Surplus of Paddy at the Farm Level in Four East Indian villages" for the year 1958-61, it is postulated that production is the most important determinant of marketed surplus. The villages covered were growing delta villages of Godavari, Krishna and Cavery. The study revealed that marketed surplus increases with holding size, simply because production increases with an increase in size-holdings. According to the authors a shift in payments from kind to cash, would have increased the demand for paddy and will also result in a rise in marketable surplus. Such a shift will also transform the agrarian sector from subsistence to commercial sector.

Mandal and Ghosh also conducted another study with data for 1960. The study entitled, "A Study of Marketed Surplus of Paddy at the Farm Level in Four East Indian villages" have taken two developed villages of West Bengal and two backward districts of Orissa, to study the behaviourial pattern of marketed surplus. The work revealed that marketed surplus increases with increase in farm size and output. Elasticity of sales with respect to size of holdings is greater than unity in each of the villages. Farmers of all size-holdings both in backward as well as developed districts offer more as marketed surplus, with an increase in total receipt of the crops, yet all farmers are left with a net balance, which can be used as stocks. Marginal propensity to hold stock was higher in backward districts in comparison to developed districts. Marginal propensity of marketed surplus rises along with holding size.

Another work conducted during the sixties was by Vyas and Mahajan on "Factors Governing Marketable Surplus and Marketed Surplus—A Study of Two Regions of Gujarat and Rajasthan". In this work it was revealed that in both the districts, marketable surplus of food crops was recorded to be a direct function of production. With respect to commercial crops small farmers sell as much as large producers sell, which is equal to their production. Fitting log-linear equations into regression models the work reveals that the elasticity of marketable surplus with respect to output is positive and less than unity for commercial crops, but greater then unity, with respect to data for superior as well as coarse cereals. An interesting revelation of the work is that the intercepts in all equations of marketed surplus is negative, implying that purchases of foodgrains dominate over zero levels of output.

Agarwal's study relating to data for 1965-66, for Etawah district of U.P. reveal that out of total production of agricultural produce 64.43 per cent was retained and only 35.57 per cent was offered as surplus. The author identified separately the factors that affect the total volume of production and factors affecting consumption. The retention and marketed surplus were functions of size-holdings. The study reveals that 51 per cent of land was owned by large farmers who contributed 48 per cent of marketed surplus. The farmers of medium sized land held 21 per cent of land, they contributed 34 per cent of surplus, whereas small farmers held 28 per cent of land, but contribute only 18 per cent as surplus. This according to the author, could be, because the second category land holders are economically better off than the small farmers.

Among the work conducted during the seventies, was one undertaken by Hati, for the Hoogly district of West Bengal. In his work, "Non-linear Marketable Surplus Functions", the author used two non-linear equations and grafted them into one. Different farm size-holdings forms the basis of plotting the graph. The results consists of three parts. In the first part of the curve upto 0.66 hectares of size holdings, marketed surplus is revealed to be negative, and the curve rises steeply upward till it cross the zero line. At the next stage, the curve flattens at 5 per cent of marketed surplus for holding size of 0.66 and 1.98 hectares. At this stage, increase in farm size has very little affect. At the third stage for size-holdings of 1.98 hectares and above, the proportion of marketed surplus rises at an increasing rate with increase in farm size and consequently, the concentration of marketed surplus is the highest at this stage.

M.V. Nadkarni in his work "Marketable Surplus and Market Dependence", deals with the production of millet in Ahmadnagar of Maharashtra. Data relates to average cross-section of 143 farm households obtained from Farm Management Survey for the period from 1969-70 to 1971-72. The author examined the trend and pattern of both marketed and marketable surplus of all foodgrains as well as for jowar, bajra and wheat separately. The study was related to the responsiveness of marketed and marketable surplus to output. The results were obtained through tabular analysis for different size classes of farm households. The results revealed that negative net marketed and marketable surplus of both jower and bajra is the smallest in two or even three size-classes. The marketable surplus was positive for all size-holdings only in the case of wheat. For jowar and bajra the proportion of marketable surplus rise sharply with holding size, though in case of wheat this trend was not evident. Elasticity with respect to output were high and above unity in case of marketable surplus, but was lower though above unity in case of gross marketed surplus. Like the experience of most other regions small farmers were engaged in distress sales, selling one commodity and buying another for their consumption.

Ashok Gulati's study which also runs on similar lines deals with 1971-72 data and reveals that marketed surplus increases in direct proportion to holding size. Gulati's study also reveals that the surplus ratio in the smaller holdings is low, and it is high among the larger size class. An important finding of this work is the lease-in and lease-out factors indulged in by small and big farmers. Smaller farmers, as they do not have much land of their own, lease-in land from rich and big farmers, who in turn lease-out their lands to small farmers. The rent for such land is paid in kind in terms of paddy. This is neither factor which reduces the quantum of their marketed surplus. In contrast, rich farmers lease-out their land and earn payment in kind increasing their quantum of surplus.

Another work conducted during the period 1971-72 was by Partha Sarathy and Kamalakar entitled, "Marketable and Marketed Surplus in Paddy and Groundnut on Small Farms" for four villages of Nellore district of Andhra Pradesh. Cross-sectional data was collected for 96 cultivators. The authors identified size of family, size of farm and total production as the determinants of marketed surplus of paddy and groundnut and used regression equations as their technique of analysis. The study revealed that marketable and marketed surplus as a proportion of production revealed a direct relationship with size-holdings for paddy, whereas marketed surplus revealed similar relationship with respect to groundnuts. Marketable surplus of paddy was 84.6 per cent in case of large-sized farms and 82.9 per cent in case of medium-sized farms, whereas it was 63.1 per cent for all size-holdings. With respect to groundnut on the other hand it ranged between 82.9 per cent on medium farms to 84.6 per cent for large ones and 83.9 per cent for the entire sample size. In case of marketed surplus of paddy it was 46.3 per cent for small farms, 56.4 per cent for medium and 63.7 per cent for large farmers. For the entire sample size it was 59.9 per cent. The study revealed that farm size and total production were the most important determinants of marketed surplus and size of family hardly had any influence either in the case of paddy or groundnut.

Among some of the works conducted during the eighties was the one undertaken by M. Upendra for the Warangal district of Andhra Pradesh during the period 1985-86. The study based on cross-sectional data collected from 320 cultivators, belonging to various size-holdings deal with the responsiveness of marketable surplus of paddy to output according to holding size and responsiveness of marketable surplus of paddy to price movements in terms of secondary data. The results of the study reveal that farmers with 2 acres of land retained a major portion of their production and released a smaller quantum as marketed surplus, whereas farmers of large holding size retained less than 50 per cent of their output and offered more than half of their produce as marketed surplus. With the exception of the smallest two size-holdings, for the rest, marketable surplus and gross marketed surplus to total output showed a positive relationship with size of farms. A considerable amount of difference was observed between marketable and gross market surplus, indicating the presence of stock retained by most farmers of various size-holdings with maximum amount for the medium size-holdings. For the first two size holdings there was however no difference between the two. Net marketed surplus is greater than marketable surplus for the first and third size groups, indicating the presence of 'distress sale'.

Another work of significance, during the corresponding period was conducted by J. Prasad for Muzaffarpur district of North Bihar with the help of both primary and secondary data. A total of 120 cultivators spread over 15 villages were selected through the method of multi-stage stratified random sampling method. Results of the study conducted through tabular analysis and regression techniques reveal that marketable surplus as a proportion of output is 44.9 per cent for foodgrains and is 46.3 per cent for rice. Gross marketed surplus is 53.8 per cent of output, out of which 52.8 per cent was for paddy. Net marketed surplus however is lower. Marketable surplus rises sharply with increase of holding size. Due to higher proportion of farmers of large size-holdings in total area and production, proportion of marketable surplus too is much higher for this group. The results of regression also reveal that both marketable and marketed surplus increase more than proportionately with an increase in output, because the elasticities are higher than unity for all size-holdings except the very small-sized ones.

Only one study conducted by the present author, relates to Barak Valley of South Assam for data during the period 1997. The work based only on tabular analysis of data according to holding size reveal that marketed surplus as a proportion of gross output, increases directly according to holding size. The lowest holding size of 0-1 hectares contribute 13.5 per cent of its gross output as marketed surplus and highest group contributes 42.4 per cent. For the valley as a whole, marketed surplus is as much as 30.1 per cent. There is however a sudden dip in marketed surplus for the size class 2.01-3.0 hectares. For the first two groups there is a considerable gap between net and gross marketed surplus, though the gap disappears for big land holdings. NMS is not negative even for the smallest groups, as in some other regions. The various factors identified as determinants of marketed surplus, are production of paddy, which was observed to be the most crucial determinants, followed by retention (though no break-up of retention was considered) and margins.

Though the present work follows the overall pattern of the above work, yet it will explore further using various regression models, the relative strength of the determinants of marketed surplus for a much later period. It will also enable the comparison of the findings of the present work with the earlier one.

All the above mentioned works on marketed surplus reveal that though a general trend and pattern of both marketable and marketed surplus can be observed for various regions of the country, in so far as it reveals that smaller size-holdings generate smaller quantity of marketable surplus, whereas bigger holding size generates larger quantum. In no region of the country however, the same set of determinants govern the surplus. The nature and extent of these determinants vary from one region to another, depending upon the socio-economic nature of the region, as well as its geographical location. All these aspects, relating to Barak Valley with its own characteristic pattern of production, remoteness and geographical location, absence of regulated markets and the in consequent impact on marketed surplus will all be explored in detail in the present work. The present study will also take into account the educational level of the cultivators and their impact on marketed surplus, which no earlier study has attempted to examine. Experience has also revealed that the total household income of the farmers and the source of major percentage of their income whether from agricultural sources or non-agricultural sources, also has an impact on the desire of the farmers to increase the quantum of marketed surplus which very few working on this area have touched upon. It has also been observed from the above studies that in most of the work on similar areas, though retention has been assigned a role in determination of marketed surplus, yet break-up of the components of retention, such as for consumption, for future sales, for payment in cash and for all other reasons have not been dealt with separately. Analysis of each of these factors may throw more light on the behaviourial pattern of marketed surplus, which the present work will attempt to examine, in addition to the determinants of the factors which earlier studies have already undertaken.

2.3 Significance of Agricultural Marketing for Disposal of Marketed Surplus

The most important channel for the disposal of marketed surplus is through the strategy of agricultural marketing. In the absence of a proper system of marketing, the surplus generated by the producers cannot reach the consumers and marketed surplus will loose much of its significance. Therefore any study on marketed surplus will remain incomplete and unconvincing without a reference to agricultural marketing. Only after the sale of the produce in the market, the entire process of agricultural production is considered to be complete. It is only when the producer is able to deliver his produce to the final consumers at a remunerative price that the process of production can be kept going. Inability to sell the produce serves as a disincentive for further production. Proper marketing strategy has two main objectives. On one hand, it aims to provide remunerative prices for the farmer, so that his interest in agriculture is retained. On the other hand, it aims to make available to the consumers agricultural produce at reasonable prices. Therefore stabilisation of prices is attempted to be achieved through the right strategy of marketing.

It needs to be noted that the system of agricultural marketing is not a static phenomenon, but a wholly dynamic one, where the interests of producers, consumers and middlemen are in constant divergence, and are hence changing continuously. Such dynamism characterises both buying and selling and involves all activities right from the time the product leaves the market till it reaches the consumers. The conflicting interests in a dynamic set-up is therefore attempted to be maneovoured in a balanced way by regulated markets. In the process the regulated system of market by involving itself in all activities from the producers to the consumers gives form utility, time utility and place utility to the agricultural produce which emerges as marketed surplus.

An efficient system of agricultural marketing aims at striking a balance between the conflicting aims of the producers, middlemen and the consumers. The producers normally aim at getting the highest price for his produce, whereas the consumers aim at consuming the maximum quantity at the minimum price. The middlemen on the other hand, aim to get the highest possible profit through commission at various stages. The correct strategy of agricultural marketing tries to synchronise the conflicting aims of all these three entities. The welfare of the farming community and the agricultural sector, therefore ultimately depends on agricultural marketing.

The system of agricultural marketing is different from marketing of manufactured items, in which case the entire product is brought for sale in the market. In case of agricultural produce, where farmers themselves consume a substantial portion of their own produce, only a certain proportion of the product is offered for sale in the market. That proportion which is offered for sale is termed as marketed surplus. This amount, unlike as in the case of the industrial sector, does not depend entirely on the level of production, but is determined by the extent of farmers own consumption, the amount of the produce that he wants to retain for payments in kind to the labourers, creditors and landlords, and quantity that is retained for seeds or for the purpose of sale at a favourable time. Unlike marketing of manufactured items, a larger quantity of agricultural produce may be sold immediately in the post harvest season, particularly by less well-off farmers, because such farmers are in need of immediate cash. At a later period, the same farmers buy from the market, may be at a much higher price for their own consumption. It is due to all these reasons that marketing of agricultural produce assumes a special significance in the study and analysis of marketable and marketed surplus.

2.4 Necessity of Agricultural Marketing

The important role of agricultural marketing notwithstanding, very little has been done by way of building up a strong marketing infrastructure in the country. Agricultural marketing was totally neglected in the first two Five Year Plans. The structure of market, which was in existence, was mainly due to commercialisation of agriculture and the result of its own dynamics of growth. The success of Green Revolution in the states of Punjab, Haryana and Western U.P. was to a large extent determined by marketing facilities. Even small and marginal farmers were encouraged to bring their produce to the markets and dispose off their surplus at remunerative prices. This enabled the total quantum of marketed surplus, to increase boosting up the process of Green Revolution even further. When small farmers are able to dispose off their marketable surplus at prices which not only covers their cost of production, but is also left with a margin, his interest in production is retained and he can even be encouraged to go in for modern techniques of production.

In the absence of establishment of regulated markets, the small and marginal farmers have to dispose off their marketable surplus to only one trader, who usually dominates the marketing activities of the villages. He not only purchases the agricultural surplus, but also provides credit and supplies other agricultural inputs to the village cultivators. These traders also indulge in the practice of supplying consumer items to the small and marginal farmers. Needless to say, inputs and consumer items are supplied at higher prices and agricultural produce is bought at a low price, totally dominating the small farmers in every aspect.

Such practices prevent the farmers from knowing the correct price prevailing in the market. Added to this, absence of storage facilities compel them to dispose of their surplus to the traders who often, in connivance with the wholesalers, pay the minimum price to the farmers. The debt obligation to the traders, compels the farmer to sell his produce to the traders at whatever price is given to him, preventing him from going to the urban agricultural marketing centers.

The small farmer as a result has always been totally dependent on the traders and never felt the need or had the money to go to the market for the sale of his produce at a higher price. Agriculture was therefore carried on a subsistence basis and there was no desire or incentive for raising production. The small producers in the process remain totally ignorant about the procedural matters relating to marketing operation, and are virtually removed from the marketing arena.

All these malpractices with respect to the disposal of marketable surplus, particularly relating to the small and marginal farmers, who dominate the Indian agricultural scenario, necessitated the formation of regulated markets where state was expected to play a dominant role. Regulated markets also aim at removing the monopoly of the trader or the middlemen and protecting the interest of the producers. By increasing the margin of the producer, through reduction of commission agents, the sense of security of the producer is increased. Increased confidence enables him to concentrate more on production and consequently he is encouraged to bring greater quantum of marketable surplus to the market where he knows his interest will be protected. It is therefore pertinent that formation of market for agricultural produce is the only answer for conducting the business of agriculture on a commercial basis.

2.5 Regulated Markets for Marketable Surplus: Implications for Developing Nations

The importance of regulated markets is unique to the Indian system, unlike as in the developed nations. The Agricultural Production Team in its Report in 1959, focused attention on the importance of such markets, when it postulated that "the development of regulation of markets be stressed especially in areas with large marketable surplus of foodgrains". In the Indian context, cooperative society, as in Soviet Russia or some other countries, for mopping up marketable surplus cannot be expected, since cooperatives have proved to be a failure in

India. At the same time establishment of producer controlled marketing boards is also difficult in India, since farmers in this country are small, fragmented and scattered. Under the circumstances, regulating market practices in the wholesale and retail markets is the only alternative, which provides a system of marketing of agricultural produce, specific to only developing nations. Malpractices, which reduce the welfare of the farmers, are removed through legislative measures. The major aim of the various Acts in this connection is to bring all parties—the producers, traders and the consumers to similar level of advantage by removing malpractices and rationalising market charges.

Unlike as in the highly developed countries like United States, Canada or Australia, developing countries cannot afford to construct huge elevators for collecting and storing agricultural produce. In contrast, in less well-off nations, direct contact between a good section of the producers and consumers is evident. This is more true for small and marginal farmers, who produce more for subsistence rather than as a large commercial venture. It is only the large farmers who mostly stand to benefit from regulated markets, where agricultural produce is exchanged in the wholesale markets, and not the former category of farmers, who cannot afford to wait for cash for so long. Therefore in most developing nations, including India, till recently the absence of proper marketing services, ungraded and unstandardised commodities, poor and unscientific packing and methods of transport, warehouses, lack of market information, unfair practices by middlemen, poor credit facilities, had been the most important obstacles to smooth marketing of agricultural produce. In fact even today, in backward regions and remote villages, such problems are only too common. The four maladjustments that characterize marketing practice in India for instance are production of agricultural produce in the wrong place, at the wrong time, in the wrong quantity and wrong quality, are attempted to be eliminated by middlemen (by providing transport, storage, sorting and grading facilities. Consequently, they undertake the usual business risk). The price for all this has ultimately to be borne by the consumers, who pay a price for the goods, plus services and the price for so called convenience (Prasad, 1989). Consequently, marketing services of this nature, do not allow agricultural markets to be perfectly competitive, particularly in developing nations. It is the natural condition and the actions of the middlemen which determine supply conditions. Net income of farmers is therefore determined by the margin that is retained by such middlemen which in the ultimate analysis determines the future course of production. Regulated markets under such circumstances in developing nations therefore are the only possible solution.

It is also important to mention here, that the traders and the commission agents cannot be totally dispensed with in the Indian agricultural marketing scenario. They are indispensable, as has been proved by various unsuccessful attempts to eliminate them altogether, from the market scenario. The Government has therefore through various legislative measures attempted to curb their malpractices. Consequently, there now exist certified Government dealers and stockists. The Government fixes the fees for their services. The important roles of the middlemen are recognised for channelising agricultural surplus to the consumers from the farmers, and also indicates (direction of the type of produce and the quantity of the same in the future) the quantity and the type of production that is to be undertaken in the future.

The tasks of regulating agricultural marketing are left to the State Governments, whereas the drafting of market legislation and its implementation is left to the Directorate of Marketing and Inspection at the central level. Though some initiatives with regard to regulated markets had been taken even prior to independence, in the post independence period, Planning Commission emphasized the vital role played by regulated markets. The Commission urged upon all the states to enact legislatures for orderly marketing of farm products and regulate agricultural markets in their respective states.

The First and the Second Five Year Plans emphasized the need for accelerating the process of regulating the marketing centres, without doing anything substantial in this regard. The Third Five Year Plan emphasized the consolidation of the functioning of the already existing regulated markets. Nine states recorded the establishment of regulated markets during the Third Five Year Plan, which was followed by the states of Assam, Kerala, Jammu and Kashmir during the Fourth and Fifth Five Year Plans. The result of this was that till the mid-sixties, 580 additional agricultural markets were brought under regulation, so that total number of regulated markets in the country stood at 1012 (Acharya, 1994). By the end of 1980 total of 18 states and four union territories witnessed the formation of Agricultural Produce Marketing Acts (Prasad, 1985).

A significant step in agricultural marketing was the introduction of certification through "Agmark" which aimed at regulating marketing practice through standardisation of weights and measures, introduction of quality standards and developing suitable infrastructure. However, success of such measures unfortunately had been extremely limited. Firstly, success rate in none of the states have been even, and secondly taking advantage of various loopholes of these Acts and Regulations farmers continued to be the victims of unfair trading practices. The malpractice was more prominent in backward states like Assam, where the implementation and monitring agencies had always been extremely weak. Due to lack of proper enforcement, deductions and charges of various forms and nature continued to exist in almost all the markets of the region. Like some other states, Assam too suffered from the shortcoming of being inadequately equipped with the means of acquiring land, planning and supervision of agricultural markets and enforcement of market regulations.

In the regulated markets, Governments played an indirect role and it was recognised as an effective tool for safeguarding the interests of both the producers and consumers. This role of Government gained further support from the findings of Raj Krishna's work which maintained that in underdeveloped countries which are of an agrarian nature, marketable surplus are highly responsive to prices.

However, experts opine that agricultural marketing in India is characterized by high degree of imperfections. Ashok Rudra for instance opines that, "the market structure of foodgrains is thus seen to be neither competitive nor optimal. It would require a singular capacity for shutting one's *status quo* in the Indian social structure to think otherwise and deny its exploitative nature" (Rudra, 1982). It is a widely maintained opinion that agricultural marketing in India is imperfect, mainly because of the vicious circle of socio-economic structure, particularly in the agrarian sector where farmers produce under extreme financial constraints and sell marketable surplus under acute distress conditions.

Markets are also imperfect due to inadequate infrastructural facilities, poor road conditions and backward technology. Lack of competition among middlemen and commission agents often obstructs any measure undertaken to uplift the condition of the farmer producer. The result of all these is as studies have revealed that village sales within villages often predominate markets and traders are patronized in this respect by landlords and money-lenders. The nineties too received priorities as far as maximisation of market surplus is concerned. The initial step in this regard was greater emphasis on domestic production for which reliance was placed on improved technology. However, generation of greater volume of marketed surplus necessitates creation of market environment for which

Government intervention was considered a necessary and the most important step. The major focus of such interventions was to increase production by providing remunerative prices to farmers, protecting the interests of consumers particularly the less well-off ones, and thereby supply foodgrains under public distribution system at reasonable rates. It was also thought extremely necessary to even out inter-season fluctuations in foodgrain supply and their consequent affect on prices, by building up buffer stocks.

The strategy that were considered necessary to achieve the above objectives were:

1. Improvement of marketing infrastructure and acceleration in the rate of establishment of regulated markets.
2. Adoption of a price policy in keeping with the demand of the economy so that farmers get an incentive to increase production.
3. Setting up of market intervention agencies for buying and selling of agricultural commodities.
4. Regulation of the activities of the private traders (Acharya, 1999).

The above measures that were adopted improved to a considerable extent the condition of agricultural marketing in India. Adequate quantum of buffer stock was built up and price stabilisation was achieved, and the margins of private traders which had always been a source of major concern was reduced considerably. Another great advantage was increased monetisation of the agrarian sector. Inspite of long years of operation a considerable portion of transaction in the rural agricultural sector was carried on the basis of barter system of exchange, due to the absence of price incentives. The measures undertaken above for increased efficiency of regulated market removed these obstacles and monetisation of the rural agricultural sector was a definite and positive improvement in this respect.

The future course of action for strengthening of regulated markets would be increasing the number of markets and bringing in more items of agricultural produce under them. This will enable the farmers to carry their produce to a nearby market instead of travelling for miles to a distant market. Apart from this, if most of the products which they produce can find a market in the regulated markets by increasing the number of products to be brought under regulated markets, other farmer-produces will be more oriented towards such markets which will enable them to reduce the level of exploitation to a large extent. The most important aspect that demands urgent attention is the regulation of margins of commission agents and their trading practices. Financial assistance in this regard has also being given by the Central Directorate of Marketing and Inspection, mostly for the purpose of grading facilities for cash crops. Assistance has also being given for the purpose of both primary as well as wholesale markets and to markets dominated by commercial crops as well as terminal markets, dealing mostly in fruits and vegetables. Notwithstanding these attempts, not only many more markets need to be regulated, but the progress of the existing ones also is not very satisfactory. In fact, some of the states in India, particularly in North East India, have still not taken any steps for the formation of regulated markets.

2.6 Structural Organisation of Agricultural Markets for Disposing off Marketable Surplus

Structure of Agricultural Markets consist of a three tier system. The first tier is the primary market or rural *haat*, where farmers sell their surplus either to the village trader or the itinerant trader Each village or groups of villages have these *haats*, which meet once or twice a week, the dates of which are known in advance. Small quantum of surplus are exchanged in these markets either for money or other items of daily use, which the itinerant traders bring for the farmers. A portion of the surplus, is also sold to the retailers, who sell them directly to the non-farm population. The remaining portion of the surplus is purchased by the intermediaries to be sold off in the wholesale market.

As already discussed, these rural primary *haats* are extremely underdeveloped and inadequately equipped with infrastructural facilities. They neither have the storage facilities, nor are they connected with proper system of road and communications. Village roads, particularly in the north-eastern region, are sometimes not fit for even bullock carts. Consequently, farmers themselves have to carry the loads on their heads and travel for long distances before reaching the *haats*. It is observed in most parts of the country that, even farmers who are able to offer a larger quantum of surplus offer them to these small traders, because they find that there is not enough margin, sell the produce to the wholesalers.

In the next tier, is the primary wholesale markets, which receives the surpluses from a wide range of rural primary markets. They have a fixed place and meet and transact daily large quantities of surpluses for even distant places. Most of these markets are located in the capitals, district head-quarters or main marketing centres of the state. The village merchants sell their produce in the secondary markets, either to the commission agents or wholesale traders. Secondary markets are also called terminal markets. In most cases big farmers, who have greater volume of surpluses sell directly to the wholesalers or commission agents in such markets.

The nature of competition and the strategy of pricing in the primary, secondary and terminal markets mentioned above depends on the number of traders, the degree of concentration of buyers and sellers, conditions of entry, and the extent of agent and product differentiation. The extent of competitive structure of the market, indicates the extent of benefit that producers-sellers may derive from the market. In backward economies and remote places, market structure is characterized by small competitive traders, who lack sufficient resources to increase the level of efficiency. The existence of a large number of traders in the agricultural marketing scenario may often be mistaken as an assurance that the producer-sellers, who dispose their marketable surplus to such traders, also receive the highest return. Some studies have revealed the existence of competition in the Indian agricultural market. However, it is maintained by others that traders have totally monopolised the Indian farmers, especially the small and marginal ones, and thus there is absence of any kind of competition in the Indian marketing scenario. In fact, efforts at ensuring adequate returns to some farmers, have often been thwarted by traders and middlemen for the fear of their margin getting reduced.

In fact, it is contended that imperfections mark Indian agricultural marketing. The village trader, who is a monopolist as far as selling consumers items to farmers are concerned, becomes the monoposonist when he purchases the marketable surplus from the farmers. This double role is further strengthened due to the total dependence of the farmers on these traders not only for the disposal of marketable surplus, but even for credit. Market imperfections, is further accentuated, since only those middlemen and commission agents with government licenses are permitted to operate. Apart from that, in most village markets, outsiders are prevented to operate due to the strong social system. Empirical reality in most of the rural markets, spread throughout the country, reveal that agricultural markets are dominated by large number of small and marginal farmers and only a few traders.

Unlike as in the developed countries, in India, market structure is not static, but varies from time to time, depending on certain factors. For instance, seasonal fluctuations of marketed surplus is indeed an important determinant. The post harvest season witnesses major spurt in supply when small farmers have no alternative but to dispose off their entire marketable surplus. It then becomes a buyer's market. During the lean period traders are keen to acquire the produce, but it is only the big farmers, who have storage capacity and are in a position to dispose off their produce, though small farmers may have more to dispose off. Consequently, sellers under such circumstances may dominate the market condition. Therefore there is nothing definite that can be said about the agricultural market structure in India, though evidence of competition as opined by a good number of scholars, appears to be unconvincing given the empirical reality of the Indian agricultural scenario.

The system of agricultural marketing in India, consists of the "task of assembling the produce from widely scattered producers and moving them to the ultimate consumers, is performed by a chain of intermediaries through which various foodgrains passes, and in the process, gain in value due to a change in time, place and form of ownership" (Subbarao). In other words marketed surplus generated by the farmers, whatever be the size of their landholdings, can reach the final consumers only through a series of intermediaries. These intermediaries are placed at different tiers of the agriculture market structure and their buying and selling activities form a chain of activities in the regulated agricultural markets.

Inspite of the steps undertaken for making the system of agricultural marketing effective, several shortcomings still characterize the system. There is for instance the maximum malpractices evident in many of the marketing yards. Even in agriculturally progressive states there is considerable amount of loss incurred during loading, unloading, cleaning, sieving, transportation and reporting of excess weights. Market yards are also characterized by excessive congestion.

There is also too much of bureaucratization in the management of such regulated markets. Competitive functioning which could have increased efficiency is not allowed to operate due to the strong associations of the traders, commission agents and other functionaries. This has also resulted in increasing the marketing costs.

The Agricultural Produce Market Committees (APMC) being the sole providers of market places for transaction of agricultural produce, have become rather complacent about providing better facilities to the farmers for efficient trading practices. They have also not been able to provide conducive conditions for other agencies to enter the market arena and provide essential services such as cleaning, grading, packing and branding. APMC has also not utilized the proceeds collected as market fee for the development of marketing infrastructure. As a result, most markets lack even the minimum marketing infrastructure.

Over and above these problems more than 27,000 rural primary markets have remained outside the purview of the development process and our study area is a victim of such deprivation and negligence. Private sectors should therefore be permitted to enter the marketing scenario so that even the backward and remote markets are brought within the wider ambit of marketing facilities. Besides private sectors may also be assigned the functions of cleaning, grading, packaging activities which are at present grossly neglected.

2.7 Significance of Marketing Infrastructure for Agricultural Marketing

Whatever be the degree and nature of market regulation for the successful marketing of agricultural produce, no commercially viable marketing practice can operate and be successful in the absence of adequate marketing infrastructure. Reference of various types of marketing infrastructure has already been made in the earlier sections, though the present section will make a detailed analysis of the same.

A number of studies have established the relationship between agricultural marketing infrastructure and success of agricultural marketing. Infrastructure increases the marketing efficiency and support the process of commercialization of agriculture by providing sustenance to agricultural production and generation of income particularly to small farmers and provides impetus to capital formation in the agricultural sector. This in turn encourages investment in this sector which is conspicuous by its absence in the Indian economy. Marketing infrastructure can forge a link between markets which are at a distance. Market integration can facilitate the operation of market forces and remove market imperfections, a serious problem characterizing markets of remote and backward places. The nature and extent of the availability of marketing infrastructure determines the difference in benefit, which the farmers get by selling their crops. Infrastructural facilities available in Indian states have been broadly categorized into two main groups. Infrastructurally advanced states and backward states. Assam falls under the category of extremely underdeveloped marketing infrastructure unlike the states of Punjab, Haryana and the southern states where such facilities are highly developed. Inadequate and insufficient infrastructural facilities are one of the most crucial factors responsible for the generation of a small quantum of marketed surplus. Marketing infrastructure can be put under two categories, one is the physical infrastructure and the other the institutional infrastructure. The former consists of road and transport, storage, electrification, grading, packing and processing. The second consists of cooperatives and other institutions to facilitate the marketing process and the price support mechanism. As far as investment is concerned, physical infrastructure initially requires large financial investment, whereas institutional infrastructure does not require large initial investment, but requires large costs for their operation and maintenance. In the absence of either type of infrastructure farmers face numerous obstacles and do not get the necessary support for the disposal of their produce. As a result they do not get any kind of incentive for the disposal of their produce due to which marketable surplus is invariably on the lower side, so that even if production rises marketable surplus may not increase concomitantly. This is therefore another reason due to which marketable surplus in remote and backward places characterized by inadequate infrastructure does not rise even if production rises. It is due to this reason, that there is a linear and positive correlation between marketable surplus and marketing infrastructure.

Marketing infrastructure is more significant in areas dominated by small and marginal farmers because it can reduce marketing costs. This in turn can reduce the disparity between rural and urban areas. Facilities provided by such infrastructure may not only increase the quantum of marketed surplus but also the quality. This is particularly because careless handling, threshing, grading and storing, packing or even transporting the produce in the absence of physical and institutional infrastructure may have an adverse effect on the quality offered for sale. Good system of grading and packaging and standardization at the farmers level, due to which post harvest losses are still as high as 7 per cent for wheat and 4.2 per cent for rice, according to a study conducted by NIAM. Losses such as these are more serious for farmers in backward and remote areas, because their degree of awareness and education is much lower in comparison to farmers of urban and developed areas.

In the Indian context, investment in marketing infrastructure was almost divorced from agricultural development strategy. It was hardly of any importance that marketing infrastructure can provide strong impetus to production and sale, which in turn can effect income distribution in favour of small and marginal farmers who dominate the Indian agricultural scenario. As a result the responsibility of marketing infrastructure was vested to the public sector. However, realizing the importance of such infrastructure for the agricultural sector, post reform period since 1991, witnessed opening up of such infrastructural investment to the private sector also. This was necessary in view of the fact that huge financial investment for such infrastructure is called for. Relying only on public investment may slacken down the pace of providing such facilities to the agricultural sector.

It is thus essential that linkage between agricultural marketing, marketing infrastructure and marketable surplus be accepted as an integral part of agricultural policy. This can not only go a long way in raising marketable surplus, but, also provide impetus for conducting the business of agriculture on commercial lines. In fact, talking about raising marketable surplus without paying due attention to infrastructure do not carry any weight.

2.8 Marketing Practices in Barak Valley

Barak Valley is characterized by a lack of any kind of regulated market for the sale of agricultural produce. Paddy which is the most important crop of this place is brought by the farmers themselves to the local markets or bazaars as they are popularly called here. Such bazaars are held on certain fixed days of the week either in some open places in the village or on the roadsides which is a regular meeting place for buying and selling of paddy. In very interior villages, the farmers instead of cash prefer other consumer items for which they may have to travel to the markets, which again are miles away from their own villages. To that extent therefore the quantum of marketed surplus is reduced, since a significant proportion of the produce is not exchanged for cash and do not come under the estimation of marketed surplus which is to be generated for the purpose of sale in the market.

Another interesting feature characterizes the nature of disposal of marketed surplus. The quantity offered for sale varies with the economic position of the farmers. Small and marginal farmers who dominate the agricultural scenario of the Valley mostly offer their produce to the money-lenders in exchange for the money borrowed from them for the purpose of cultivation. Hence, such farmers are neither interested in knowing the market price nor can they afford to conduct agriculture on commercial lines. Secondly, there are those farmers who have large size holdings but conduct agriculture as an additional business to their regular profession. Most of their family members after acquiring education have shifted to urban areas mostly to Government jobs. Hence, they neither have the inclination nor the time to invest for the marketing of their produce on commercial lines. They depend totally on the middlemen who come to this group of farmers and purchase the produce directly from them paying the cost of transporting the produce to the market themselves. This category of farmers too are not interested in conducting agriculture on commercial lines since they consider agriculture production as a supplement to their other sources of income. There is the third category of farmers who own large lands and also possess sufficient education and conduct agriculture on totally commercial lines. Such farmers are aware of the market prices and release the produce for sale in the market accordingly. They are also the ones who have no other sources of income and agriculture constitutes their only source of income and are hence more inclined to conduct it on the basis of profit motive.

References

Acharya, S (2004): *"State of the Indian Farmer"*. Ministry of Agriculture, Vol. 17, GoI, New Delhi.

Archarya, S.S. (1994): *"Marketing Environment for Farm Products: Emerging Issues and Challenges"* Presidential Address, 8th

Annual Conference of Indian Society of Agricultural Marketing, Patna.

Bhattacharjee, J.P. (1960): "Changing Characteristics of the Flow of Foodgrains Surplus from the Farmer". *Agricultural Situation in India,* Vol. 14.

Directorate of Marketing, (1968): *"Working of Regulated Markets in India-Regulated Markets"* Volume II, Ministry of Food and Agriculture, GoI, Nagpur.

Gulati, Ashok (1980): "Distribution of Marketed Surplus of Agricultural Products by Operational Holdings Groups in India 1971-72." *Indian Economic Association* Vol. 1.

Hati, Ashok (1976): "Non-linear Marketable Surplus Function *"Economic and Political Weekly,* Vol. XI, No. 27.

Krishna, Raj (1965): "The Marketable Surplus Function for a Subsistence Crop—An Analysis with Indian Data" *The Economic and Political Weekly,* Volume 17.

Mandal and Ghosh, H.G. (1968): "A Study of Marketed Surplus of Paddy at the Farm Level in Four East Indian Villages" *Indian Journal of Agricultural Economics* Vol. 48, No. 3.

Nadkarni, M.V. (1980): *"Marketable Surplus and Market Dependence in Millet Region"* Allied Publishers Pvt. Ltd.

Narain, Dharam (1961): *"Distribution of Marketed Surplus of Agricultural Produce by Size-level of Holdings in India 1950-51"*, Institute of Economic Growth, Occational Paper No. 2, Asia Publishing House, Bombay.

Parthasarathy, P.B. and Kamalkar, M. (1975): "Marketable and Marketed Surplus in Paddy and Groundnut of Small Farms" *Indian Journal of Agricultural Economics,* Vol. 30, No. 3.

Patnaik, Utsa (1975): "Contribution to the Output and Marketable Surplus of Agricultural Products by Cultivating Groups in India 1960-61", *Economic and Political Weekly.* Vol. X, No. 52.

Prasad, J. (1989): *Marketable Surplus and Market Performance,* Mittal Publications, N. Delhi.

Raj, K.N., Sen A. and Rao H. (1988): *"Dharam Narain Studies on Indian Agriculture"* Oxford University Press, New Delhi.

Rudra, Ashok (1982): "Myth of Marketing Efficiency" in *Indian Agricultural Economics,* Allied Publishers, New Delhi.

Sengupta, Keya (1998): "Behaviourial Pattern of Marketed Surplus in Barak Valley of South Assam "*Agricultural Situation in India.* October, GoI, New Delhi.

Shukla, G.S. (1999): "Planning for the Development of the Rural Markets" *Encyclopedia of Agricultural Marketing,* Mittal Publications.

Singh, S.K. (1999): "Agricultural Marketing in India: Issues and Options", *Encyclopedia of Agricultural Marketing,* Mittal Publications, New Delhi.

Subbarao K. (1978): "Rice Marketing System and Compulsory Levies in A.P." *Op cit.* Talukdar, K.C. "Efficiency and Equity of Farm Prices in Assam", *Indian Journal of Agricultural Economics,* XL (3).

Upendra, M. (1990): *"Marketable and Marketed Surplus in Agriculture"*, Mittal Publications, New Delhi.

Vyas, and Mahajan, H.H. (1966): "Factors Affecting Marketing Surplus and Marketed Supplies—A Case Study of the Regions in Gujarat and Rajasthan", *Artha Vikas,* Vol. 2, No. 1.

3

Background of the Study Area and Objectives of the Present Study

3.1 Introduction

The entire procedure of marketing is a very complicated system, which is often beyond the comprehension of small and marginal farmers. The complexity of the entire system appears to be more puzzling for cultivators of remote and isolated areas such as Barak Valley who do not have much experience regarding market regulation, market practices and various legislations guiding such practices. Successful marketing strategy is a combined effort of institutional, technological, financial and managerial factors, all of which are conspicuously marked by their absence in most of the less developed areas. Experiences of such places reveal that marketing implies development of a few primary assembling centres at certain convenient places which are used for assembling, distribution and exchange of goods. These goods mostly consist both of paddy and other crops which farmers produce, and also consumer goods which the cultivators consume. Traders play a dominant role in these markets and they often ignore the interest of the cultivators both as producers as well as buyers.

The quantum of marketed surplus, in remote and backward regions therefore does not always depend upon production and other economic factors, but also upon the socio-economic condition of the regions, particularly in backward areas dominated by small and marginal farmers who carry on farming on a subsistence basis. When such cultivators are confronted with numerous barriers and obstacles for profitably disposing off their produce, they have no alternative but to be totally dependent on the middlemen. Economic barriers emerge in the form of roads and communication, long distance from the main marketing centres and the inability to adapt new technology of agricultural production. Added to such problems, are also the socio-economic factors, which may not only limit their degree of awareness regarding marketing practices, but may also push down labour output as well as capital: labour ratio in agriculture. As a result, such trends may compel the farmers to be confined to inefficient productive technology and to small size holdings.

An important reason for the continuation of acute poverty in the remote areas is the fact that cultivators in most cases do not get their due return from their produce. The traditional socio-economic set up in such places prevents commercialization of agriculture. Distress sale is therefore a characteristic feature of such farmers. The existence of 'semi-feudal constraints' in many parts of agricultural sector of our country only perpetuates such problems. Though the zamindari system has been abolished in rural agricultural sector, the practice of rich land-owners leasing out land on rent to the cultivators, who are mostly small and marginal, is still prevalent in most places. The result of the prevalence of this type of practice is that large sized land-owners with vast land conduct agriculture in an inefficient manner since they are not able to manage the land sufficiently. This is inspite of the fact that they possess the ability to conduct production and sale in an efficient way. They are neither interested in investing in the agricultural sector nor in getting remunerative prices for their product. As a result, marketed surplus does not increase as much as warranted by their economic condition. On the other hand, marginal farmers lack the ability to invest in their land, and though they desire to sell their produce at remunerative prices, due to extreme poverty they often conduct production more efficiently than large farmers. Thus, marketed surplus cannot increase either on the part of rich farmers or even on the part of the poor farmers as much as it should. Unremunerative prices reduce the margin and discourage further investment in agricultural sector, helping the continuation of mass poverty. Consequently, the sector which has to play a dominant role in the development of rural economy experiences a sluggish growth. As a result the economic growth of the entire region slackens.

3.2 Agricultural Scenario

All these issues relating to marketing will be examined for the plain region of south Assam, known as Barak Valley. The Valley consists of three districts, namely Cachar, Karimganj and Hailakandhi with geographical area of 3786 sq km 1809, sq km and 1327 sq km respectively (Census, 2001). Brahmaputra Valley on the other hand occupies the northern part of the state and comprises 71.7 per cent of the total area of the state, whereas Barak Valley occupies only 8.9 per cent area of the state.

Agriculture occupies the major occupation of the people particularly in the rural areas which has almost 91 per cent of rural population. The contribution of agriculture to Gross District Domestic Product is 39.34 per cent, though the sector employs nearly 70 per cent of the population in this sector. The average size holding in the valley is much smaller than the Indian average being as low as 1.62 hectares. According to Agricultural Census of 1990-91, 53 per cent of the holdings are in the size group of below 1 hectares. This is followed by the percentage of holding of the size group of 1-2 hectares which is 23.85 per cent. Number of holdings decline sharply in the holdings of 2-3 hectares and 4 and above, being only 18.80 per cent and 4.26 per cent of total holdings respectively.

Cultivation of paddy occupies a dominant place in the cropping pattern of the state and rice is the staple food of the people of the region. While the cultivation of paddy was 91.64 per cent in 1971-72, it was 93.39 per cent in 1998-99. The crop cultivated in the region are pulses, rape, mustard, potato and sugarcane. As far as paddy is concerned, there are mainly two crops grown in the year, namely the winter crop called the *boro* cultivation and the autumn crop called the *kharif* crop. The *boro* crop is the most important crop of the year.

Knowledge of agricultural marketing practice in any region therefore calls for a thorough understanding of the socio-economic structure of the study area. The condition of agricultural productivity and its constraints needs to be highlighted, which may therefore enable us to capture the essence of the problem. It is with this aim in view that we give a brief socio-economic background of our study area.

3.3 Socio-economic Condition of Barak Valley

Though in the pre-partition days the Valley was highly prosperous economically, but has now been affected in an extremely adverse manner due to the partition of the country. The Valley has been almost totally cut off from the mainland and is connected by means of roadways which is the main means of communication of the Valley. Communication with Assam and other states of the north east such as Tripura, Manipur and Mizoram do exist, but being connected mainly through mountainous roads are often disrupted due to heavy rains and landslides. This is the one most single crucial factor which has retarded the economic growth of the region and increased poverty, particularly in the rural areas, because marketability of any kind of local product under such conditions is unremunarative and therefore serves as a great disincentive to any further improvement.

It is therefore not only the remoteness of the region, but the extremely poor road and communication infrastructure that has prevented any form of industrialization worth mentioning. As a result agriculture apart from service sector, trade and commerce in the urban areas constitute the main source of livelihood of the major section of the people. However, agriculture too cannot be conducted on commercial lines due to extreme poverty and lack of adequate marketing facilities. However, given the proper incentives of marketing agricultural products, particularly that of paddy, could have catered to the local demand of the States of Manipur, Mizoram and Tripura for whom paddy is the staple food.

Data for 1997-98, reveals that the net area sown in Barak Valley was 224.0 thousand hectares, which accounts for only 32.43 per cent of the total area of the Valley. The gross cropped area for the corresponding period is 299.1 thousand hectares. Cropping intensity for the region was therefore 134 per cent as against 145 per cent for the state as a whole during this period. Size of holdings of agricultural land in the Valley is extremely low in comparison to most other agriculturally advanced states in India. This prevents mechanization of agriculture, added to which is already the existing problem of poverty among farmers. The average size holdings in the state is only 1.62 hectares as against 3.85 hectares in Punjab and 4.49 hectares in Gujarat. According to the Agricultural Census of 1990-91, the highest number of land holdings of 53.09 per cent is of land which is less than 1.0 hectare. There is a sharp decline thereafter, for holdings between 1-2 hectares, which is only of 23.85 per cent, followed by 18.80 per cent for land holdings of 2-4 hectares. This is again followed by a sharp fall of 4.26 per cent for large sized holdings of 4-10 hectares. Holdings above 10 hectares are extremely few, being as low as 0.32 per cent.

It is therefore evident that large sized holdings in the Valley is extremely low and agricultural production is dominated by small farmers which has significant impact on productivity and marketability of agricultural produce since paddy constitutes the principal crop grown in the Valley and is cultivated three times in a year.

3.4 Demographic and Socio-economic Profile of the Valley

Productivity of agriculture, consumption and sales is determined to a large extent by the demographic pressure as also its trend. The demographic profile of Barak Valley displays some distinctive features which is worth taking note of, since it may have some definite impact on the trend of marketable surplus that is generated in the Valley. The total population in the Valley according to the 2001 Census was 29.89 lakhs. Though the total population according to 1991 Census was much less and stood at 24.91 lakhs, the decadal growth in the post partition period from 1941-1951 displayed a clear tendency of a sudden jump of 23.80 per cent and experienced a steady upward trend thereafter. Such a tendency is evident of the fact that partition of the country witnessed a sudden migration into the Valley from across the border, which has continued unabated, though the rate of growth has now suddenly declined. A major section of the migrant population settled down in rural areas. Consequently, there is a heavy pressure of population in the rural areas and on land in those areas, where almost the entire population depends upon agriculture either directly or indirectly. The dominance of rural population is also evident from the Census Report of 1991, according to which 91.4 per cent of the population of the Valley is in rural areas, and the remaining 8.6 per cent in the urban areas. The rural bias of the population is higher than that of the state, which is 88.9 per cent, whereas it is only 73.0 per cent for India as a whole. It therefore reveals that the significance of agricultural production, consumption and sale of agricultural produce, particularly that of paddy, which is the major crop cultivated in the area, is much more important for the economy of the Valley than other parts of the country. In fact, dominance of population in rural sector also reveals that agriculture is the major source of income as well as economic development in the Valley.

This section of the population fall back on agriculture, take some land and small scale paddy cultivation which becomes the main source of their livelihood. Tenancy cultivation in rural areas is therefore mostly conducted on subsistence basis as a result of which they are neither attempted to be modernized nor conducted on commercial lines. Such demographic structure is an important factor contributing to the large scale existence of small and marginal farmers with small holdings. Absence of large size holdings, which may have the ability to raise marketable surplus is mainly due to large scale migration, heavy population pressure and consequent scarcity of land. It is therefore not surprising that the Valley experiences one of the highest figures for density of population of 448 persons per square km according to Census 2001. This is much above the figure for the state which is only 340 per square km, or even the country as a whole which stands at 324 per square km. With such high population density and such a significant percentage of the population still engaged in agriculture, there is over crowding in this sector, with all its related adverse effects on the generation of adequate quantum of marketable surplus. For similar reasons it is not surprising that all the Census Reports relating to this area reveal a higher percentage of marginal workers in rural areas in comparison to urban areas, the level of unemployment being less than that of urban areas. This implies a greater pressure of population on land in rural areas and the resultant adverse impact on agricultural productivity. It is due to this reason that more than 70 per cent of the population in the Valley are engaged in the agricultural sector, meaning that majority of the people depend on agriculture for their livelihood. A break up of the work force in the primary sector reveals that the highest percentage of 40.99 per cent according to 1991 and 2001 Censuses respectively are engaged as cultivators, which further substantiates our hypothesis of greater population pressure on land.

Absence of industrialization in the Valley, coupled with lack of modernization in agriculture and heavy population pressure on land, results in lowering the per capita income in the Valley, which is therefore much lower than both the state's average as well as the national average. Though there is heavy dependence on agricultural sector, yet the contribution of the sector to Gross District Domestic Product is only 40 per cent.

Production in the agricultural sector is marked by the absence of modern technology. Even the use of fertilizers per hectare is much below the national average, resulting in lowering the productivity of land. Irrigation which is the next most important contributory factor for raising agricultural productivity is in extremely poor condition hampering all types of agricultural progress. There is practically total absence of private system of irrigation. As for the Government contribution, barely 2 per cent of the total cropped area is covered by irrigational facilities. What is of even greater concern is that, out of this meagre percentage almost the entire amount is unutilized, sometimes the utilization ratio is as low as 5 per cent. Agriculture without the help of irrigation is always low and unpredictable and is exposed to all kinds of marketing hazards. This is more true for a region like Barak Valley, which witnesses heavy rains during several months in the year with frequent occurrence of floods. Destruction of crops is therefore quite a common feature in the Valley. On the other hand, absence of rainfall during the rest of the year do not permit production to continue on a regular basis.

Therefore inspite of adequate volume of rainfall, uneven distribution of rainfall throughout the year prevents uniform production in the agricultural sector with its adverse effect on the generation of marketable surplus.

The Valley also witnesses certain socio-economic traits which if capitalized in the right manner may bring about rapid growth of its economy and improvement in the quality of life of its people. For instance, two out of the three districts of the Valley namely, Cachar and Karimganj districts experiences high literacy rates of 68.4 per cent and 67.2 per cent respectively. Such high literacy rates stands very favourably against the 65.4 per cent literacy rate of India according to the Census Report, 2001. This feature of the Valley is a very significant trait when one is aware of the fact that the record of the Valley with respect to most other economic indicators is highly unfavourable. Even the record of female literacy rate in the Valley is better than in comparison to the national scenario. Whereas the record for all-India for female literacy is 54.2 per cent, it is 56.9 per cent for Barak Valley. The Valley can therefore be considered to have a strong social sector at least as far as education is concerned. This advantage can go a long way in improving the performance of the agricultural sector both in terms of its productivity as well as in terms of its marketability.

Along with high female literacy the Valley is characterized by a very favourable sex ratio, which is another indication of a positive socio-economic structure of the place. This ratio according to the latest Census Report is 941 as against 933 for the country as a whole and 932 for the state of Assam. Among the three constituent districts, Cachar district records the most favourable sex ratio of 945, followed by 944 for Karimganj and 933 for Hailakandi. Added to this is also the fact that female work participation rate in all the three districts is also highly satisfactory (Paul R., 2003). In other words taking an overall view, the study reveals that gender discrimination in this area is much lower as against the all India scenario.

3.5 (i) Objectives of the Study

Against the profile of the Valley given above, the following would be the main objectives of the study.

The first objective of the study would be to examine whether marketed surplus responds significantly to changes in agricultural production which can thereby reflect the degree of agricultural prosperity of the region. Such a relationship may reveal the crucial fact that due to extreme poverty of the farmers, a rise in the price of agricultural commodities means more income for the farmers. In years of poor harvest, when prices are higher, a greater quantum of crops may be realized for marketing, provided cash, is the first requirement of the farmers. On the contrary, lower prices in years of good harvest means lower income for the farmers and therefore less may be offered for sale inspite of higher production.

In view of the pre-dominance of small and marginal farmers, the next objective of the study will be to examine whether marketed surplus is related to size-holdings of farmers.

The other objective of the study will be to examine whether the perverse behaviour in sales is reflected in the consumption pattern also. Therefore an important objective of the study would be to investigate the responsiveness of marketed surplus to price changes as well as in the level of production. In view of the dominance of paddy cultivation and the fact that rice is the staple food for majority of the people of this region, attention will be focused on the behaviour of marketed surplus of only this most important crop of the region.

In almost all studies, attention is always concentrated in examining the relative importance of the economic factors for the determination of marketed surplus. However, for a poverty stricken region, socio-economic factors particularly literacy rate can be an important determinant factor for marketed surplus. The next objective of the study will therefore be to evaluate the relative role of education in determining marketed surplus.

(ii) Hypothesis of the Study

1 Higher production need not always lead to higher marketed surplus. Higher production may be absorbed in satisfying consumption requirements of the small and marginal farmers whose marginal propensity to consume is high, so that higher production may result in higher consumption and not in higher marketed surplus. On the other hand, if the consumption level of the farmers is already high, higher production in most cases will lead to higher marketed surplus.

2 The second hypothesis which follows from the first would thus be that higher the level of consumption lower would be the quantum of marketed surplus and lower the volume of consumption, higher the quantum of marketed surplus.

3 Higher prices of paddy results in lower level of marketed surplus, especially among the small sized holdings, since the amount of cash required by the farmers may be met by selling a smaller quantum. In contrast, lower prices results in higher volume of marketed surplus, since more has to be sold to acquire the required amount of cash.

4 Higher level of education among the farmers may lead to higher production, since a literate farmer is more aware than an illiterate farmer regarding the best use of agricultural inputs, use of institutional credit and all other various facilities that leads to

higher production. Higher volume of marketable surplus will result from such an act since a literate farmer is more informed about the market conditions and the various ways of conducting his business profitably. He is also less susceptible to be exploited by the middlemen in comparison to an illiterate farmer. As a result, a greater proportion of profit may accrue directly to the farmer rather than to the middlemen, encouraging the farmers to offer more for sale.

3.6 Methodology of the Study

Data for the purpose of the study has been obtained mainly from the primary sources and supplemented wherever necessary by information from secondary sources obtained from Basic Statistics of North Eastern Region, Economic Survey of Assam and Handbook of Economics and Statistics. For the purpose of collecting the primary data, information has been obtained through the interview method by using the stratified multi-stage sampling method. For this purpose, the three districts of the Valley, that is Cachar, Karimganj and Hailakandi have been made the first tier of the survey. Each of these districts have been divided into blocks out of which 25 per cent of the blocks have been selected. From each of the blocks thus selected, twenty five per cent of the villages have been chosen which formed the next stage of the sample. From the selected villages the next stage was the selection of twenty five per cent of the household on a purposive basis so that the cultivators with four different categories of land holdings were of the following type: 0-1 hectare, 1.01-2.0 hectares, 2.01-3.0 hectares and 3.0 hecatres and above. In view of the fact that there are not very many holdings of very large size we have not made any further categorization. The total sample size for the study has therefore been about 300.

The information thus obtained has first been classified and tabulated in terms of the objectives of the study according to different holding sizes of the households. Analysis of the tables has been made and the trend and pattern of marketed surplus of the various size-holdings has been studied taking the determinants of such surpluses as a whole and also according to holding sizes. From the conclusions of such an analysis important determinants of marketed surpluses in the Valley have been identified. On the basis of these determinants, models for the study have been formulated in an attempt to know the exact quantitative relationship of marketed surplus and their determinants as well as the relative weights of these determinants. On the basis of these estimated results of the models, conclusions for the behavioural pattern of marketable surplus for 'Barak' Valley has been derived.

3.7 Conceptual Framework of the Study

This section will be devoted to the definition of some of the important terms and concepts that will be used in the course of this work. The most important among this is the concept of **marketable surplus**. It is the quantum of agricultural produce that is available for sale in the market, after the farmers meet the various obligations relating to the production, sale as well as that of his own requirements. The farmer after retaining a part of the paddy produced for his own consumption, for payments in kind to the labourers, landlords and creditors, retain a portion of the produce as seeds to be used in the next season as well as for sales. After meeting all these requirements he is left with a certain quantity of the produce. It is therefore the excess of output over various forms of requirements of the farmers that is available for sale in the market. The on farm utilization of the produce is extremely important for the determination of marketable surplus because whatever is the residual after meeting all the above mentioned requirements is the quantity actually available for disposal in the market. It is the *"ex ante"* concept, because the total quantum available for sale may not be actually sold in the market. Marketable surplus is therefore the total production minus total retention. If various modes of payments are made in cash rather than in kind the total quantity of marketable surplus will surely increase.

Marketed surplus on the other hand is an "ex post" concept. It is an objective term because it refers to the quantum that is actually sold in the market during a particular period of time. This is in contrast to marketable surplus which is available for sale, but may not actually be sold. Marketable and marketed surplus therefore are not identical, and a totally different set of factors determine the two variables. However, it needs to be highlighted that marketed surplus is influenced by marketable surplus, though the reverse need not be the case. Due to the unfavourable price in the market, whatever is available for sale may not be actually sold. In such cases marketed surplus is lower than marketable surplus. Experiences have also revealed that, due to acute financial need, especially among the small and marginal farmers, they may sell more than the actual amount available for sale. This is attained by cutting down on their own consumption needs. Such sales are termed as distressed sale. Under such circumstances, marketed surplus are higher than marketable surplus. Thus marketed surplus may be equal to, less than or even be higher than marketable surplus. Wastages and various form of payments in kind to agents, middlemen or traders in the course of transporting the produce from the place of production to the place of sale, are some of the other factors that do not allow marketable and marketed surplus to be equal. It is therefore pertinent to highlight that some of the factors that determine marketable surplus are different from the factors that determine marketed surplus, though there are also a good number of common determinants as well.

The other concepts that are of relevance for the purpose of the study are **gross marketed surplus and net marketed surplus**. The former term refers to the total amount that is offered for sale in the market. The amount includes the quantum of distress sale that is offered by small and marginal farmers and is therefore not included under marketable surplus, but is included under gross marketed surplus. The quantum of distress sale is the amount that would have been retained for consumption. The farmers after selling this quantity repurchase them again at a later period from the market, often at a much higher price. For the purpose of policy considerations as far as procurement prices are concerned, it is the gross marketed surplus which is more relevant. It reveals the total quantity that can be procured for sale in the market. Net marketed surplus is the genuine quantity of the produce that is actually marketed. Small and marginal farmers who indulge in distress sale, are often under the compulsion of repurchasing the crops from the market for their own consumption at a later date, at a price which is different from the price at which they had originally disposed off the products in the market. This quantity in reality should have been included under retention and not under marketed surplus and hence the quantum has to be deducted from marketed surplus. The difference between the two is thus defined as net marketed surplus. The distinction between 'gross' and 'net' marketed surplus assumes significance only with respect to foodcrops, particularly staple foodcrops. This is because retention for the purpose of self consumption is relevant not for cash crops but only for foodgrains.

Retention is an important term which will be used frequently in the course of the study. It is an important determinant of both marketed as well as marketable surplus. Retention in simple words imply, that portion of the produce which is not offered for sale in the market. Retention is crucial only with respect to foodgrains, particularly the staple food like paddy and wheat, which the farmers may consume themselves or are used for payments in kind to all types of payment receivers, who also use it for their own consumption purposes. Cash or commercial crops cannot be used for the purpose of direct consumption in this way and therefore retention may not assume the same degree of importance with respect to such crops. As the present study deals exclusively with marketed surplus of paddy, retention therefore assumes importance. The cultivators keep a significant proportion of paddy for their own consumption to be used for the entire family during the course of the entire year. The amount that is retained by small and marginal farmers and farmers of large sized-holdings differ substantially in nature. The small farmers are often in financial crisis and are therefore in acute need of cash. They are therefore often seen to retain less and sell off immediately in the post harvest season at whatever price they are able to obtain. For their self consumption they may buy later, of a variety which may be inferior to the one they themselves have sold in the market. Studies (Mathur and Ezekiel, 1961) have revealed that for poor farmers cash requirement is their first priority. Therefore when prices in the market are favourable they sell a small quantum and retain a larger quantum for their own consumption, since their marginal propensity to consume is extremely high. By selling a smaller quantity at a higher price they are able to get the required amount of cash and therefore the quantum of retention rises under such circumstances. Rich farmers on the other hand retain a higher quantum when market prices are low, so that they are able to sell at a later date when prices are higher. Such farmers often sell more when the quality of their produce is inferior, so that the quantum of retention under such circumstances may be low, and purchase superior variety of paddy from the market at a higher price. Volume of retention by these farmers also rises when price in the market is unfavourable and declines with a rise in the market price.

Apart from the above mentioned factors, retention is also made particularly in a non monetized economy. Such practices are common in remote places where payments in kind are to be made to the landlords for leasing out lands to cultivators for payments to labourers or even to creditors from whom the small and marginal farmers take loan for the purpose of cultivation as well as for their own personal reasons. Payment in kind is also made to the village traders in exchange for offer of various types of consumer items of daily use to the farmers. A certain quantity of the produce is also retained to be used as seed for the next season. In places where large scale production is carried on a commercial basis, rich farmers also retain a significant proportion of the produce for selling at a favourable price, time and place at a later date. Retention has a broad perspective and therefore considered an important determinant of marketed surplus.

References

Basic Statistics of North-Eastern Region: Various Issues, North Eastern Council, Shillong.

Census Reports: 2001 GoI, New Delhi.

Economic Survey of Assam: Various Issues, Directorate of Economics and Statistics, Government of Assam, Guwahati.

Mathur, P.N. and H. Ezekiel (1961): Marketable Surplus Function of Food and Price Fluctuations in a Developing Economy. *Kyklos*, Volume 14., No 1.

Mazumdar, A.P. Acharjee and Bhattacherjee, J. (1998): *"Statistical Profile of Barak Valley"* NECAS, Silchar, Assam.

Sengupta, K. (1998): "Behaviourial Pattern of Marketable Surplus in Barak Valley of South Assam", *Agricultural Situation in India*, October, GoI, New Delhi.

Statistical Handbook of Assam: Various Issues, Directorate of Economics and Statistics, Government of Assam.

4

Factors Determining the Pattern of Marketed Surplus

4.1 Introduction

In this chapter we shall examine the information obtained through the collection of primary data on marketable and marketed surplus, production of paddy, consumption and sales behaviour of farmers and other related variables for the various cropping seasons. The information obtained through the questionnaires have been classified and tabulated for the three constituent districts of the Valley, namely Cachar, Karimganj and Hailakandi as well as for the Valley as a whole. The information is based on cross sectional data obtained from farmers selected on the basis of multi stage purposive sampling method. The sample farmers were classified into four groups according to the size of their farms. In view of the fact that the Valley is conspicuous by the absence of very large size farms, the farmers had to be put into four broad groups according to land holdings. In the following section, we shall analyse the behavioural pattern of marketable and marketed surplus according to size of land holdings and their determinants in an attempt to assess the factors that shape the behavioural pattern of the marketed and marketable surplus.

The analysis would be extremely important for the policy makers as the findings will enable them to identify the crucial factors that determine the generation of surplus. It is essential to note that different factors may display different degrees of significance and importance in different regions or states, which is determined by locational factors, socio-economic condition of the farmers, extent of population in the farm sector and many other factors, which vary from place to place.

It is quite possible that one or two factors may be dominant in one region, whereas all factors may dominate simultaneously in the others, even within the same region. It is also possible that similar factors may not operate with the same degree of strength for different size-holdings. Some factors may play a dominant role among the farmers of small size-holdings, while others may be crucial for large size holdings. As a result generalizations of the conclusions on such surpluses on the basis of using the same variables may become extremely unrealistic. This calls for a detailed analysis of the factors at micro level for all size-holdings.

4.2 Marketable and Marketed Surplus of Paddy

In this section we shall first examine the behaviourial pattern of marketable and marketed surplus of paddy of the farmers of the Valley and its constituent districts. We shall also examine whether the trend is in keeping with the trend in other regions. For the purpose of this work, marketable surplus has been estimated by deducting total retention from total production. The retention constitutes the amount kept for self consumption, for seeds, inventories for the forthcoming season and payments in kind to labourers and creditors. Marketed surplus on the other hand is estimated simply by estimating the total amount of the produce sold in the market and the net marketed surplus is the actual sales minus repurchase of paddy by the farmers for self consumption. The estimation thus assumes the following form:

1. Marketable Surplus = Total Production – Retentions.
2. Gross Marketed Surplus or Actual Sales = Quantity actually sold.
3. Net Marketed Surplus = Actual Sales – Repurchase of paddy.

It needs to be mentioned here that marketing of agricultural produce was almost negligible in pre-independence period in Barak Valley. The situation worsened further in the post-independence period when the country was partitioned. Partition of the country affected transport and communication system of Barak Valley much more adversely than in any other part of the country. The region was left totally isolated and its locational disadvantage became the biggest hurdle to any serious effort for the marketing of agricultural produce. Non-commercial form of exchange of agricultural produce became the dominant practice. Added to this, was also the problem of high level of poverty of the rural peasantry and heavy indebtedness, all of which combined to form the main constraints to proper development of agricultural marketing system. Consequently, there has not yet been much evidence of successful marketing of foodgrains, and the local nature of marketing of foodgrains reflected the non-commercial character of the agricultural sector of the economy.

It is against this background of agricultural marketing in the region that we shall analyse the behavioural pattern of marketable and marketed surplus in Barak Valley from the data presented above. Table 4.1 reveals that 43.91 per cent of the output produced in the Valley is offered as marketable surplus. The smaller two size-holdings fall much below the average, whereas the larger two groups are much higher than this average. It is also revealed that marketable surplus increased in direct proportion to the size of land holdings, unlike the 'U' pattern curve of marketable surplus as maintained by Narian. It is the lowest among the farmers of size-holdings of 0-1 hectares, revealing the highest level of poverty among the various groups of farmers. Subsistence farming is the way of life and a major portion of the produce which is as high as 85 per cent (since they offer only 15.29 per cent as marketed surplus) is used either for self-consumption or for the payment of debt in kind to the creditors. Payment to labourers is not common among this group of farmers, since the farmers along with their family members work on the field themselves and do not hire wage labourers in an attempt to reduce their cost of production. Among the farmers with large size-holdings, the volume of marketable surplus as a proportion of production increases steadily with holding size and the proportion of retention decreases. This is mainly due to the fact that though in absolute amount, the quantum of surplus retained for consumption and other purposes increases with the increase in the proportion of output, it reveals a declining tendency, due to larger volume of output. It also needs to be noted that as farm size increases owners and farm labourers, constitute clearly two distinct groups. The owners do not cultivate the land themselves, but hire labourers to cultivate their farms who are often paid in kind instead of cash. As a result, retention on this account, reduces marketable surplus among this groups of farmers, much more than the small size-holdings. Apart from this, as owners are unable to supervise their own farm themselves, due to the large size of the farms, there is considerable amount of wastage as well. Consequently, marketable surplus gets reduced. This could be a possible reason, due to which the surplus of the largest size-holdings do not increase in direct proportion to size of their holdings. It needs to be highlighted here that though the marketable surplus as a proportion of output of the larger size-holdings can be comparable to other states, but that of the lower size-holdings is much below that of most other states, revealing the extreme level of poverty of the farmers of this category. It also reveals that agriculture is carried on at a totally subsistence level, and the surplus is generated with an effort to be sold in the market in order to get the minimum cash required by them.

Table 4.1: Gross and Net Marketed Surplus of Paddy by Size- Holdings

Size holdings	*0-1 hect.*	*1.01-2.0 hect.*	*2.01-3.0 hect.*	*3.01 hect. and above*	*Total*
Marketable surplus (in quintals)	647	1776.2	2985.4	5758.6	11167.2
Marketable surplus as p.c. of output	15.29	32.86	50.47	58.27	43.91
P.C. share of the class in total marketable surplus of all classes	5.79	15.91	26.73	51.57	100

Source: Estimated from Primary Data.

For similar reasons, when we examine the percentage share of the respective groups in the total marketable surplus, it is revealed that the smallest land holders offer the minimum quantum, whereas the largest ones offer the major portion of the marketable surplus amounting to over 78 per cent of the total.

4.3 Gross and Net Marketed Surplus

It is therefore pertinent to focus attention at this juncture, to the behavioural pattern of gross marketed surplus or the actual amount of the surplus sold in the market. The entire amount of the marketable surplus which is available for sale, may not be actually sold in the market. There may therefore be a considerable amount of gap between marketable and marketed surplus which may arise due to various reasons according to different size-holdings. In the Table 4.2 below we present the figures on gross marketed surplus and net marketed surplus as well as the percentages of such surpluses to total output produced by the farmers.

Table 4.2: Marketed Surplus of Paddy by Size-Holdings

Size Class	*0-1.0 hect.*	*1.01-2.0 hect.*	*2.01-3.0 hect*	*3.01 hect. and above*	*Total*
Gross marketed surplus (in quintals)	567	1336.6	2184	3506.6	7594.2
G.M.S. as p.c. of output	13.40	24.73	36.92	35.48	29.86
Marketed surplus	80	440	801	2252	
Net marketed surplus (in quintals)	21.9	1047.6	2155	3480.6	6705.1
NMS as percentage of output	0.52	19.38	36.43	35.22	26.36
Purchases from market	545 (96.1%)	289 (21.6%)	29 (1.32%)	26 (0.074%)	889
P.C. share of the class in total marketed surplus of all classes	0.133	15.62	32.14	51.91	100

Source: Based on Field Survey Data.

Since marketed surplus represents actual sale of paddy by the farmers, difference between marketable and marketed surplus may reveal several tendencies of sale, purchase and stock behaviour of the crop. Excess of marketable surplus over marketed surplus indicates that stocks are held by the farmers to be released in the market, either when the price is more favourable or stocks are held for emergencies or unforeseen future. On the other hand, when marketable and marketed surplus are equal, it indicates the farmers are not in a position to hold back stocks, due to the urgent necessity of cash. A composition of the figures for marketable and marketed surplus for different size-holdings in our case reveal that unlike marketable surplus, marketed surplus as proportion of output increases with size-holdings but declines marginally thereafter in the highest holding size of 3 hectares and above. The average marketed surplus for the first two categories of land holdings works out to be 19 per cent of gross output and for the higher two size-holdings it works out to be 36.2 per cent. It is therefore true that this conforms to the findings of other similar works, that small farmers have to meet various financial obligations related to their cultivation and hence are compelled to sell a smaller quantity in the market. The farmers belonging to large size-holdings due to their stronger economic position are able to produce a higher quantum of paddy and also do not need to retain the produce for various forms of financial obligations. As a result they are able to sell more than their counterparts having small land holdings. The fact that marketed surplus declines marginally or has a tendency to become stable with higher size-holdings do not follow the well known findings of either Utsa Patnaik who maintains that marketed surplus increases in direct proportion to holding size, or the findings of D. Narian according to whom marketed surplus takes the shape of 'U' curve decreasing initially with increase in holding size but increasing thereafter.

A comparison of marketable and marketed surplus for the various size-holdings reveal that the former exceed the latter for all size-holdings, unlike the farmers with respect to other states, where the two surpluses tend to be equal for the smaller farmers, due to distress sale or inability to hold back stocks either due to financial compulsion or lack of space. It is true that the difference between the two is almost insignificant in case of small farmers but increases with farm size and assumes a significant proportion among large size-holdings. Presence of distress sales among farmers of small size-holdings is already discernible. The extremely small amount of stock held by them may be due to the fact that because of inadequate marketing facilities they are unwilling to hold a larger proportion as stock, to be able to sell their produce in the future. Larger volume of stocks held by farmers of large size-holdings however, indicates that agriculture is conducted not on subsistence basis, but on commercial lines. Stocks are held with the major aim of increasing profitability of the farmers. However, inspite of these findings it needs to be noted that marketable surplus as a proportion of total output for all size holdings in the Valley is much lower in comparison to similar situations in other states, where agriculture is conducted on a commercial basis. The situation is more serious in case of small farmers. It may therefore transpire from this, that agriculture in Barak Valley is still not conducted on totally commercial lines, and the generation of adequate quantity of marketable surplus leaves a lot to be desired.

Distress sale by the farmers is indicated by their purchase from the market or other farmers after the sale of their own produce. Farmers in order to receive cash sell their produce immediately after the harvesting season. However to meet their own consumption requirement or seeds for the next season, they again repurchase paddy from the market. Hence marketed surplus minus the purchases from the market amounts to net marketed surplus. Examination of Net Marketed Surplus (NMS) reveals that it has a tendency to increase in direct proportion to size-holdings in absolute terms.

It is observed from Table 4.2 above that the farmers of the two smallest size-holdings repurchase the highest quantum of paddy from the market or from the other farmers, after they sell their own produce in the market. The quantum of repurchase amounts to 545 and 289 quintals or 96.1 per cent and 21.6 per cent of marketed surplus respectively for these two groups. This clearly reveals the acute amount of distress sale indulged in by the poor farmers. For the smallest size holdings of 0-1 hectares, whereas marketed surplus is 567 quintals, NMS is only 21.9 quintals, and for the 1.01-2.0 hectares marketed surplus is 1336.6 quintals and 1047.6 quintals is the NMS. These farmers sell their produce immediately in the post harvest season when prices are extremely low and buy later, often at a higher price from the market. It may however, be mentioned here that there is no record of negative marketed surplus among these farmers. Negative marketed surplus arises when the amount of repurchase from the market exceed the amount that is actually sold in the market. This is a common practice among small and marginal farmers in some other parts of the country.

Among the farmers of large size-holdings, it is observed that there is only a negligible quantity of purchase from the market. This could perhaps be the purchases of those farmers who purchase very superior quality of paddy which is not produced in the Valley. It could also be that some quantity could be purchased due to lower price, whereas they dispose off their own produce at a much higher price, when market price is favourable. This behaviour therefore does not indicate the practice of subsistence farming, but the sole objective of such practices is higher margin and profitability which forms the basis of agricultural marketing. This experience among farmers of large size holdings differ from the other states, where such farmers do not make such purchases from the market. The reasons for this kind of behaviour in other states may be sought in the fact that production is carried on an extensive basis on a large scale with the practice of modern system of agricultural production, unlike as in the case of the farmers of this Valley. The farmers of this Valley are economically weak, both in terms of quality as well as quantity of resources. Distress sales indulged in by farmers conducting agriculture on a subsistence level is also termed as forced sales, because there is all likelihood that such surpluses may be converted into negative marketed surplus. It is for this reason that marketed surplus of the rich farmers belonging to large size-holdings is termed as positive marketed surplus, because normally such farmers do not indulge in repurchases from the market. Whatever amount is sold in the market is the actual marketed surplus. In our study we have examined the forced sales or forced marketed surplus by the amount of repurchases from the market. This amount is the highest among the farmers of the smallest size holdings and decreases sharply among the farmers of large size holdings, revealing the fall in forced sales and the proportionate rise in the economic prosperity. These findings have important implications for procurement policies.

4.4 Marketable Surplus and Retentions

It is evident from our discussion above that the extent of retention is one of the crucial factors that determine the volume of marketable surplus. Experience suggests that retention by small farmers is the highest, with the result that their surplus tends to become very small. In contrast, retention by the big farmers is much smaller, due to which the quantum of marketed surplus is also higher. It needs to be mentioned here, that in absolute amount, the quantum of retention among rich farmers may be much higher than the poor farmers. However, as a proportion of total output (since the volume of production among the rich and economically viable farmers is much higher) the percentage of surplus appears to be a small one. This enables them to offer a higher proportion as marketable surplus. The production level of the poor has always been on the lower side in all states, including that of Barak Valley, so that even if they have a smaller quantum of retention, it appears to be a large proportion of the agricultural produce. It is therefore evident, that, apart from the volume of retention the volume of production is the other most important factor governing the volume of marketed surplus. In fact, according to Krishna Raj and some other scholars, production is the most certain and definite way of determining marketed surplus. However, we will first examine the volume of retention and its relationship with marketed surplus according to size holdings.

Table 4.3: Consumption and Repurchase of Paddy by Farmers according to Holding size

Size Class	*0-1.0 hect.*	*1.01-2.0 hect.*	*2.01-3.0 hect*	*3.01 hect. and above*	*Total*
Consumption of paddy (in quintals)	1721.6	2052.9	1470.8	1616.8	6861.1
Consumption as a p.c. of production	40.69	37.98	24.86	16.36	26.98
Consumption per capita (in quintals)	2.46	2.49	2.82	2.84	2.63
Consumption per household (in quintals)	19.79	22.31	24.11	26.95	22.87
Amount of paddy purchased from the market (in quintals)	545.1	289	29	26	889.1
P.C. of purchase from the market to total consumption	24.05	12.34	1.93	1.58	11.47

Source: Based on Primary Data.

Retention may be for various purposes. Consumption by the farmers is the most important component of retention. Apart from consumption the other component of retention is for seeds. Most farmers keep aside a part of their production to be used as seeds in the next season, though farmers who are well off, purchase the HYV seeds from the market. Payments in kind (paddy) to wage labourers and creditors also form a part of the retention. Wastage due to harvesting, threshing, handling, transportation should not be overlooked, as this proportion of production does not find its way to the market. In the table 4.4 below we present the total retention and the various components of retention of the different size holdings in the Valley. We have first taken up the most important component of retention, which is consumption, shown in Table 4.3. In terms of the actual quantity of paddy consumed during the course of one year, the Table 4.3 reveals that it is the second category of size holding of 1.01

hectares—2.0 hectares that record the highest consumption of 2052 quintals. The highest size holding of 3.0 hectares and above record the lowest quantum of consumption. There is no definite pattern of relationship that can be established between land size holdings and the total quantity of paddy consumed. The reason could lie in the differences in the number of family members of the farmers of different size holdings. However, examination of consumption as a proportion of total production clearly reveals that the percentage is inversely related to size of land holdings. As size holding increases, the proportion of consumption goes down, whereas 40.69 per cent is the consumption of the lowest group only, 16.36 per cent is the consumption of the highest group. The reason for this kind of behaviour may be the differences in the level of total production. The quantum of production of large size holdings is obviously much more than the holdings of small size. However it is interesting to mention here that when we analyse such values of production for per capita and per household, it is much more than the smaller size holdings. It is further interesting to mention, that when we analyse the values for per capita and per household consumption, it is found that the values increase directly in proportion to size of land holdings. Though the consumption per capita varies marginally and ranges between 2.46 to 2.84 quintals per capita, the variation is much wider with respect to consumption per household, which ranges between 19.79 to 26.95 quintals per household. This behaviour is a revelation of the fact that the consumption level of the poor farmers is not higher, but in fact lower than the poor farmers. As a proportion of production, consumption levels of the poor farmers appear to be large, since their production level is low. In fact, lower average level of consumption of the farmers conducting farming at a subsistence level, may imply that such farmers are not consuming at the optimum level. Any increase in the level of production is likely to result in a rise in the level of consumption by the farmers, instead of a rise in the level of marketed surplus. This is further confirmed by the highest level of repurchases of paddy by farmers belonging to small size holdings. This only indicates that any rise in production may only reduce the quantum of purchase from the market so as to maintain the same level of consumption and may not result in an increase in the volume of marketed surplus. However, what is very pertinent is that, even for the smallest farmers in the Valley marketed surplus is not negative, unlike the small and marginal farmers in most other parts of the country where marketed surplus becomes negative when the quantum purchased exceeds the quantity offered as gross marketed surplus.

What therefore transpires is that farmers belonging to small size holdings devote the maximum amount of their paddy produce for the purpose of consumption, which declines quite sharply with the increase in size holdings.

Analysis of the pattern of consumption also reveals the necessity to examine the family size, and the structure of the family of the farmers of different holding sizes. This will enable us to evaluate the nature of consumption and the possible trend for the future pattern of consumption.

The size of the family that is the number of members in the family is often cited as an important determinant of marketed surplus. It is hypothesized that higher the number of family members, more the consumption and therefore more the retention and hence, less the marketable surplus. In other words marketable surplus of respective size holdings is inversely related to the number of members in the family. In the case of our study area, it is revealed from Table 4.4 that the number of family members is the lowest in the lowest size holdings.

The number varies from around 8 members per family as against almost 10 for the highest size holding. The number rises for the second category of size holding and declines for the third group once again. It is therefore evident that

Table 4.4: Dependents in the Family

Size Class	*0-1.0 hect.*	*1.01-2.0 hect.*	*2.01-3.0 hect*	*3.01 hect. and above*	*Total*
Marketable surplus (in quintals)	647.00	1776.20	2985.40	5758.60	11167.20
Marketable surplus as p.c. of output	15.29	32.86	50.47	58.27	43.91
Mean size of population per household (in number)	8.05	8.93	08.56	09.50	08.71
No. of children (No. of child population to total population of the group)	268.00 (38.29)	284.00 (34.55)	191.00 (36.59)	192.00 (33.68)	935.00 (35.77)
No. of old people who do not work in the agricultural farm	52.00	80.00	33.00	49.00	214.00
P.C. of old people	07.43	09.73	6.32	08.59	8.19
Number of dependents	320.00	364.00	224.00	241.00	1149.00
P.C. of dependents on working population	45.71	44.28	42.91	42.28	43.96
No. of people engaged in cultivation	182.00	202.00	127.00	120.00	631.00
P.C. of population engaged in cultivation	26.00	24.57	24.33	21.05	24.14

Source: Based on Primary Data from Field Survey.

the family size neither behaves proportionately with size holdings of farms nor is it the highest among the small size farms and lowest among the large size holdings, which can elicit any possible explanatory behaviour pattern of marketable surplus. This once again lends support to our earlier conclusions that marketable surplus of smaller size holdings is low not due to their high level of consumption or due to large family size and consequent higher propensity to consume. Marketable surplus is low perhaps due to the fact that such farmers are compelled to dispose off a larger share of their limited output because of the urgent requirement of cash.

Table 4.4 above also reveals, the proportion of dependents or the number of family members, who are consumers, but do not contribute in any way directly towards the purpose of production. The dependency is estimated as the number of children below 10 years and the proportion of old age people who are above 65 years. The ratio is the highest among the lowest size holding ranging from 45.71 per cent among the group below 1 hectare to 42.28 per cent among farmers with 3 hectares and more. Examining the structure of dependency, it is revealed that the number of children is the highest among the lowest size class, but lowest among the highest size holdings. This may imply that there is a tendency for a rise in the growth rate of population among farmers of small size holdings. In contrast, the number of old people is the highest among the farmers of second category land holdings. All these features may not affect marketable surplus directly, but is expected to affect the behavioural aspect of marketable surplus in the future, by influencing per capita production and per capita marketable surplus.

The other component of retention are the amount of the crops kept as seeds for the next sowing season, amount kept as inventories to be sold in the future or for consumption purposes as well as the amount paid in kind to the wage labourers and to the creditors.

Table 4.5: Marketable Surplus and the various Components of Retention

Size Class	*0-1.0 hect.*	*1.01-2.0 hect.*	*2.01-3.0 hect.*	*3.01 hect. and above*	*Total*
Net marketable surplus as p.c. of output	0.52	19.38	36.43	35.22	26.36
Wage payment and debt repayment (in quintals)	1537	944	938	1829	5248
P.C. of total output	36.09	17.46	15.85	18.50	21.97
Retention for future consumption (in quintals)	268.7	530.6	426.8	532	1758
	(66.29)	(49.45)	(32.26)	(18.15)	(30.67)
Retention for future sale	80	439.6	801.4	2252	3573
P.C. to total retention	19.74	40.97	60.57	76.82	62.33
Retention for seeds	56.6	102.7	94.8	147.4	401.5
P.C. to total retention	13.96	9.57	7.17	5.03	7.00

Source: Estimated on the basis of Field Survey.

Perusal of Table 4.5 reveals that 5248 quintals or 21.97 per cent of the total produce is used for wage and debt payments in South Assam. Table 4.5 further reveals that, the lowest as well as the highest category of land holdings use the maximum proportion of their output for payments in kind. This is the highest among the largest groups which is as high as 1829 quintals, since they have to depend entirely on hired labourers, as they themselves do not cultivate the crops. Consequently costs on this account which are implicit among small and marginal farmers as they themselves cultivate their own lands become explicit as far as the well off farmers are concerned, since they have to make the payments to the labourers. Though 6.66 per cent of the farmers (Table 4.9) of the latter category do borrow from the money-lenders, the payments are made mostly in cash and not in terms of the crops. The situation however is the reverse in case of the small farmers belonging to the 0-1 hectare land holdings. They do not make any kind of payments for wage labourers as the family members contribute their own labour in the field, but 33.33 per cent of them borrow from the money-lenders and relatives, who have to be repaid not in cash but in kind. For the two extreme categories of farmers, this reduces the quantum of marketable surplus generated by almost 36.09 per cent in case of 0-1 hectare and 18.50 per cent in case of 3 hectares and above category land holdings. Table 4.5 for obvious reasons it forms a significant part of total production as far as small size holdings are concerned. For the other two groups of 1-2 hectares and 2-3 hectares, the proportion works out to be 17.46 per cent and 15.85 per cent respectively. For both these categories, this is a combination of wage payments and debt payments. For the second group, debt payments exceed the wage payment, whereas for the third group, it is the reverse. It therefore transpires that payments in kind for meeting production cost reduce substantially the volume of marketable surplus generated in each size class.

Retention for the purpose of future consumption constitutes another important determinant of marketable surplus generated. The entire region retains about 37.67 per cent of the current output or 1758 quintals for the purpose of future consumption till the next season. Though in terms of percentage of total output the amount decreases in direct proportion to the increase in size holdings, but in terms of absolute amount the second and the fourth category of land holdings record the highest quantum of 530 and 532 quintals respectively. The reason for this could be that these two groups also record the highest number of family members as well as the highest proportion of children in the family, due to which, by way of security they keep a substantial amount of the produce for future consumption.

A part of the retention is also meant for the purpose of future sale, when the market price is more favourable. During the harvesting season a significant proportion of the produce is offered by all the farmers, due to which the price is often low. Large and economically viable farmers who have sufficient storage facilities, and who do not require immediate cash through the sale of their produce in the immediate post harvest season are able to retain a substantial portion of their produce during the harvesting season itself. Such farmers are able to sell the produce at a higher price during the lean season when prices are higher. Consequently, the retaining capacity of small and marginal farmers is lower and that of the large farmers much higher. This tendency is clearly evident from the perusal of Table 4.5, from which it is revealed that retention for future sale increases in direct proportion to the size of land holdings, in this Valley. The amount ranges from a marginal amount of 80 quintals to 2252 quintals.

It is interesting to mention here that even those farmers with less than one hectare of land holding, retain a small amount for the purpose of future sale, an interesting experience which is not evident among the farmers of small size holdings in most other parts of the country. For South Assam as a whole about 3573 quintals or 14 per cent of the total produce is held back from the market. However, such a tendency is a part of the commercialization of agriculture which is necessary to provide incentive to the farmers not only to increase production but also for marketing of their produce. On the whole therefore, it is evident that retention for future sale constitutes the highest proportion of retention and reduces marketed surplus in a substantial manner.

Most farmers keep a part of their produce, to be used as seeds in the next season. On the whole only 7 per cent of the total retention is kept for this purpose, indicating that this component of retention does not affect market arrival in any substantial manner. It is clear from table 4.5 that though in terms of absolute quantity, the amount of paddy kept for seeds, increases in direct proportion to the size of land holdings, the percentage ranges from 13.96 for the lowest land holding to 5.03 for the highest land holdings. The reason for this behavioural trait could be sought in the fact that the rich farmers can also afford to purchase HYV of seeds from the market, whereas, poor farmers are not able to afford such purchases and hence have to depend on their own produce for seeds to be used in the next harvesting season.

Taking an overall view it is evident that the factors that reduces the generation of marketable surplus on an preliminary investigation emerges to be the quantum that is retained for the purpose of consumption, followed by the amount that is retained for the purpose of wage and debt payment. This is then followed by the amount that is kept as retention for the future. Among the items for the purpose of future retention, the amount kept for the purpose of sale in the future is followed by the amount for the purpose of future consumption.

4.5 Production of Paddy and Marketable Surplus

Among the factors affecting marketable surplus, production is the surest and the most definite determinant, a fact which is supported by evidences drawn from almost all major studies on marketable surplus. An increase in the volume of production will surely result in the emergence of a high quantum of marketable surplus, other things remaining the same, just as fall in production due to a crop failure or poor harvest results in generating a small volume of marketable surplus. Investment is made in the agricultural sector, with the sole intention of getting a high return. High return can only be ensured when productivity and sales increase due to higher investment through proper marketing channels. Among the numerous factors responsible for lower volume of marketable surplus in the agriculturally backward areas one of the most crucial is the low volume of production. It is with this aim in view that we present below in Table 4.5 the pattern of production of paddy in the Valley according to size holdings, along with per capita production and other related variables, in order to assess the relationship between production of paddy and marketable surplus.

Examination of Table 4.6 reveals that total production of paddy increases in direct proportion to the size of land holdings. Production however, does not increase proportionately to size holdings. The holding of 3 acres and above records the highest level of production which is almost 133 times that of the lowest size holdings and 67 times that of the preceding size holding. The reason could be the highest amount of investment coupled with higher acreage of cultivated area of all the farmers belonging to this group. For similar reasons, the share of the various groups of land holdings also varies in direct proportion to the size of the lands.

The difference between per capita production and per capita marketable surplus, which depend on the size of the family, may highlight the potential surplus that can be generated and the amount out of total production that is retained and not offered for sale. Both these amounts increase positively with size holdings. The reasons for this

Table 4.6: Marketable Surplus and Production of Paddy according to Size Holdings

Size Holding	*0-1.0 hect.*	*1.01-2.0 hect.*	*2.01-3.0 hect.*	*3.01 hect. and above*	*Total*
Production	4230.6	5404.9	5915.4	9882.2	25433.1
P.C. share of the group to total production	16.63	21.25	23.36	38.26	100
Production per capita	23.25	26.76	46.58	82.35	40.31
Production per household	48.63	58.75	96.97	164.70	84.78
Production per hectare	48.44	38.50	42.89	35.74	39.60
Cost of production per quintal	176.09	176.15	163.65	175.38	172.94
Cost of production per hectare	8530.40	6782.26	7018.57	6267.37	6849.02
Marketable surplus per capita	0.92	2.10	5.72	10.10	4.27
Marketable surplus per household	7.44	19.31	48.94	95.98	37.22
Marketable surplus per hectare	7.41	12.65	21.64	20.82	17.39
P.C. share of the class in total marketable surplus	5.79	15.91	26.73	51.57	100

Source: Estimated from Field Survey.

can be sought in the fact that production is directly related to size holdings and marketable surplus is inversely related to size holdings and therefore also the volume of output. It needs to be mentioned here, that the average size of family influences per capita output and marketable surplus. The number of family members per household in this Valley is higher than most other states, due to which per capita output increases with size holdings and marketable surplus per capita decrease even further. Higher number of family members in the family compels them to hold more by way of retention, due to which the per capita marketable surplus show a drastic fall in comparison to per capita output. The difference between the two per capita values increase sharply with size holdings, which may be due to an increase in the number of family members which increases with the size of land. The desirability to sell at a higher price rises so that a higher margin may be retained. Therefore farmers with large holdings have the potentiality to offer much more as marketable surplus since they offer only a very small proportion of their output as per capita marketable surplus. In comparison, though the smallest size holdings offer the least volume, in terms of absolute value, as far as marketable surplus is concerned, yet in comparison to the large size-holdings, they perform much better and offer the amount which almost matches their potentiality. For this region of South Assam as a whole, marketable surplus is more than eight times lower than per capita output. It is therefore clear, that though production draws the broad contours of marketed surplus, but a wide gap still exists between the two, due to the existence of numerous factors including the acreage under production.

It is interesting to note that the per capita output is the highest, being as high as 48.44 quintals per hectare in the case of the lowest size holdings and lowest of 3574 kgs per hectare in case of the largest size holdings, when one would have expected just the reverse kind of behaviour. The reason for this kind of behaviour of output per hectare could be due to the fact that farmers belonging to small land holdings do not hire wage labourers but work themselves on the field. Consequently, being their own land or land cultivated on hired basis, they put in the optimum labour, maximizing the level of productivity, inadequate and insufficient use of modern technology notwithstanding. This reduces wastage and enables productivity per hectare to be much better than large size holdings, where economically resourceful farmers do not work on the fields themselves, but are dependent on wage labourers. As a result they get neither the optimum amount of effort from hired labourers nor can they ensure minimization of wastage in terms of time, resources and space. Therefore, it is only natural that owners of large sized land holdings, often use modern technology and have irrigation facilities and have much higher potentiality for raising productivity. Though output per hectare, is the highest for the smallest land holding, marketable surplus per hectare is the lowest. Highest proportion of retention by this group for self consumption appears to be the only explanatory factor. Surplus per hectare increases till the third group of land holdings, but declines with 3 hectare and above category of land holdings. The third category of land holdings appear to be doing quite well, with the highest per hectare surplus and second best performance in terms of productivity per hectare.

As a proportion to total output, marketable surplus of the respective holding size, a steady increase in quantum in direct proportion to size of land holding is recorded. While for the size holding of 0-1 and 1.01-2.0 hectare the proportion of surplus to total is much lower than their respective proportion of surplus to total output for the size holdings of 2.01-3.0 hectares and in the case for the highest size holding of above 3 hectares. The quantum of retention of the respective groups clearly emerges as the governing factor for this kind of behaviour.

On the whole it therefore transpires that, though larger land generates more surplus, yet they have much higher potentiality to generate much higher quantity of surplus. Small size-holdings perform relatively much better and with some effort can record better performance in terms of marketed surplus.

Analysis of Table 4.7 reveals that the use of modern technology improves directly with an increase in the size of land holdings. This is mainly due to the fact that farmers belonging to large holdings are economically in a position to make more investments. As a result, production too reveals a rising tendency along with size of land holdings. The entire Valley is marked by the absence of any irrigation facility. The impact of irrigation is more evident when we examine the percentage of micro irrigation facility. The highest percentage of farmers using this facility belongs to the third category of land size holding. It is this size holding which performs much better in terms of marketable surplus. However, the use of fertilizers per quintal among this group is the lowest and thereby the percentage of farmers using chemical fertilizers is also the lowest among this group. There is also a clear evidence of a rising trend of use of HYV seeds along with the rise in size holdings, due to which as discussed earlier, retention for the purpose of seeds, decreases with increase in size holdings.

For a perceptible rise in marketable surplus, along with marketing facilities, it is equally important to lay greater stress in raising the level of production, particularly for large size holdings. In this Valley, upgrading the level of production in the sector through capitalist transformation of agriculture, through private sector investment has been possible only to a limited extent. In the absence of any

Table 4.7: Marketable Surplus and Production Techniques according to Size Holdings

Size Holdings	*0-1.0 hect.*	*1.01-2.0 hect.*	*2.01-3.0 hect.*	*3.01 hect. and above*	*Total*
P.C. of farmers using wooden ploughs	95.40	85.87	80.33	85.0	87.33
P.C. of farmers using tractors/power tillers/pump sets/harvesters	41.38	77.17	83.61	86.66	70
P.C. of farmers with private micro irrigation facility	9.19	7.61	19.67	16.66	12.33
Amt. of chemical fertilizers used (in kg.)	2241	4903	5248	13127	25519
Amt. of fertilizers used per quintal of output (kg.)	0.53	0.91	0.89	1.33	1.00
Amt. of fertilizers used per hectare (kg.)	25.66	34.93	38.05	47.47	39.74
P.C. of farmers using pesticides/insecticides	37.93	46.74	50.82	66.66	49
P.C. of farmers using chemical fertilizers	55.17	79.35	73.77	91.68	73.66
P.C. of farmers using HYV seeds	19.54	29.35	32.79	51.66	31.66

Source: Estimated from Field Survey Data.

industries in this area, agricultural sector is devoid of any inflow of capital either from industrial or tertiary sector. Production has also been adversely affected by the total absence of any public sector capital formation projects. The Valley is a typical example of a victim of regional disparities, due to the provision of farm sector subsidy, even the benefits of higher procurement prices cannot be availed by the small and marginal farmers as their crops are taken away by the middlemen, due to lack of awareness about procurement prices and other added problems of selling the product directly in the market. Added to this, is the constant uncertainty faced by such farmers due to frequent price fluctuations in the Valley. Such practices results in the non recovery of the cost of production even in the case of bumper production. All these factors prevent investment in this sector resulting in lowering of output and the resultant marketable surplus in the long run.

4.6 Behaviourial Pattern of Marketable Surplus and Margin from the Sale of the Produce

As discussed earlier, gross marketed surplus and net marketed surplus are different from marketable surplus. The entire amount offered for sale may not be actually sold off because of various factors. The factors governing marketed surplus, gross as well as net are different from the factors governing marketable surplus. In the present section we shall examine the factors that determine gross as well as net marketed surplus through tabular analysis and attempt to discern a pattern for the same. With this aim in view we shall first take up the price prevailing in the market for paddy and the margins retained by the farmers as the most crucial determinants of marketed surplus.

Perusal of Table 4.8 reveals that the price at which paddy is sold in the market is Rs. 521 per quintal in the Valley. The farmers of the first two groups obtain a price which is lower than the average, whereas farmers of the two larger size holdings of 2.01-3.0 hectares and 3.0 hectares and above obtain a price which is higher than the average. The difference between the mean market price and the price at which the farmers belonging to the smallest size holdings sell their produce is the highest; the farmers in most cases selling at price much below the mean market price. This indicates the poor bargaining powers of the farmers. It is perhaps due to the poor bargaining power, poverty and the urgency of obtaining immediate cash which compels them to sell at whatever price is offered to them. Lower remunerative prices may act as a serious deterrent not only to higher production, but even for the generation of marketable surplus. The information in the table further reveals that prices per quintal obtained by farmers increase in a linear proportion to holding size. It may therefore be contended that prices have both a forward and backward linkage with marketed surplus. Just as lower price reduces marketed surplus, lower marketed surplus also has negative impact on price. Price of paddy therefore emerges as an important determinant of marketed surplus.

Prices obtained in the market clearly determine the margin obtained by the farmers, which is nothing but the difference between the production cost per quintal and the price obtained through the marketing of the produce. The margin is Rs. 44.94 per quintal. The farmers of the two small holdings sell at a loss, the loss being higher for the smallest size holdings of only Rs. 107.67 per quintal and Rs. 32.48 for the second group. Margins which are negative are a clear indication of higher cost of production incurred by the farmers and production below the subsistence level. This is extremely important for the policy-makers to take note of, because it indicates that poor farmers need immediate assistance and the benefits of subsidy are appropriated mostly by rich and economically viable farmers rather than the actual farmers who are needy. Inadequate marketing

Table 4.8: Pattern of Marketed Surplus and the Price of the Paddy

Holding Size	*0-1.0 hect.*	*1.01-2.0 hect.*	*2.01-3.0 hect*	*3.01 hect. and above*	*Total*
Gross marketed surplus as percentage of output	13.40	24.73	36.92	35.48	29.86
Net marketed surplus as p.c. of output	0.52	19.38	36.43	35.22	26.36
Mean price at which paddy is sold (Rs. p/quintal)	473.00	513.00	542.00	554.00	521.00
Marketing charge (Rs. p/quintal)	12.35	8.23	5.54	5.59	6.54
Marketing cost as percentage of total cost	0.93	1.14	1.23	1.12	1.12
Percentage of farmers who sell in the market	41.38	25.00	18.03	13.33	26.00
P.C. of farmers selling for middlemen/rice millers/big merchants	28.74	50.00	90.16	91.66	60.33
Mean distance from the market (km)	2.98	3.44	3.05	4.05	3.38
P.C. of farmers selling in the post harvest season	45.98	39.78	16.39	18.33	31.00
P.C. of farmers selling in mid season	19.54	34.78	63.93	56.66	40.66
P.C. of farmers selling during lean season	3.45	15.22	55.74	70.00	31.00
P.C. of farmers aware of the market price	28.74	35.87	67.21	75.00	48.00
Average expected price at which farmers want to sell the produce (Rs. p/quintal)	628.00	633.00	654.00	708.00	656.00
Mean price at which farmers purchase from the market (Rs. p/quintal)	546	545	551	550	548
Margin per quintal (Rs. p/quintal)	-107.67	-32.48	97.47	12.17	44.94
Margin per household	-5235.86	-908.09	9451.93	19956.87	3809.72
Margin per hectare	-5216.08	-250.49	4180.15	4329.98	1779.79

Source: Estimated from Field Survey Data.

facility is surely a reason for this as there is no system of paying to the farmers the right procurement price in an attempt to safeguard their interest and ensure a higher margin. Benefit of a constant rise in procurement price goes mostly to the rich farmers. In fact, small farmers are not even aware of the latest procurement price. This happens either due to the lack of awareness, inadequate informational channel or lack of education. Even if some of them may be aware of the prices, but due to the hassles of marketing, marketing cost and time constraint the necessity of immediate cash they are compelled to sell at an extremely low price and even at a loss.

The Table 4.8 further reveals that, farmers belonging to larger land holdings have a positive margin, which is clearly due to their higher bargaining power, capacity for retention, storage facility and their awareness about the market price and their overall sound economic position. However, it is interesting to note that while Rs. 12 is the margin of the farmers belonging to land holdings of 3 hectares and above, Rs. 97 is the margin of the 2.01-3.0 hectares land holdings. In other words, this category of land owners perform in a better way than the highest category of land owners. For the same reason they also offer the highest proportion of their output as marketable surplus so that one may contend that margin and proportion of marketable surplus offered are highly correlated. The lower margin of highest category of land may also be due to the fact that such farmers may be conducting farming as a side business and a supplement to other main sources of income. They may therefore not be keen to conduct farming on a purely professional basis, but yet continue to farm since they might have inherited land as an ancestral property. This enables as well as encourages them to lease out a considerable portion of their land. Highest margin of the third category of land holding may also be explained by the lowest cost of production per quintal. Greater efficiency, lower level of wastage, higher professionalism also paves the way for a higher level of margin. These factors could be the main driving forces for increasing production and productivity and hence marketed surplus in the future.

Percentage of margin obtained by the farmers is determined by a number of factors. The chief among them is the time of the year when the product is sold in the market. When the surplus generated is sold in the immediate post harvest season prices are generally on the lower side. Farmers especially the less well off ones who need immediate cash both to meet their production cost obligations, repayment of debts and for other payments as well as to meet the various needs of the family are under a compulsion to sell their produce immediately in the post harvest season at whatever price is offered to them. They can neither afford to wait for a better remunerative price in the future or are either aware or interested to know the market price, nor do they have the storage capacity to retain the produce and sell the same at a later date when prices are higher. It is due to this reason that they not only get a low price but get a low margin as well. Lower margin in turn discourage generation of marketed surplus on a large scale. Lower margin also prevents ploughing back capital for raising production through various forms of investments. There is therefore a vicious circle between lower margin and a lower quantum of marketed surplus. It is exactly for the opposite reason that farmers of large size holdings are able to hold back stock and sell at a time when prices are favourable. From Table 4.8, therefore, it is clear that such a trend exists among the farmers of South Assam. Table 4.8 reveals that small and marginal farmers belonging to the two small size-holdings sell the maximum amount of their produce in the immediate post harvest season. About 45 per cent and 39 per cent respectively of these two size holdings sell their produce in the immediate post harvest season. In contrast, (see table 4.8) the farmers of the third and fourth category land holdings earn the highest margin, since they offer the minimum amount among all categories of farmers during this period. This indicates that they conduct agriculture on a commercial basis and marketing is taken as a serious business. It is therefore evident that profits can be raised through the sale of paddy by releasing them in the lean season. Building up the storage capacity for this purpose is no doubt an important determinant, examination relating to which will be made later.

It is for similar reasons discussed above that the maximum proportion of this category of farmers accounting to almost 40 per cent offer their produce during the mid season when prices begin to rise. This is a factor explaining why this group manages to enjoy the highest margin by the sale of their paddy.

However, in the lean season, when prices are highest, 31 per cent of farmers of all size holdings offer their produce in the market. Out of this, 70 per cent of the farmers, of the largest size holdings, the highest among all the groups offer their produce and only 3.45 per cent of the lowest size holding have similar behaviourial pattern. Such wide range of variation in selling pattern and time is the most important explanatory variable explaining the differences in the margin among different size holdings. The number of farmers belonging to the third category of land however is the highest in number offering paddy during the lean season. Lack of storage capacity could perhaps be the reason, as only 19.67 per cent of the farmers of this category have storage facility. This implies that all other farmers can at best hold back the stock till mid season, beyond which holding stock would mean greater financial loss to them. Highest number of farmers belonging to the 3 hectares land holding amounting to 25 per cent has storage facility due to which highest number of farmers of this group sell during the lean season. However, notwithstanding all these facilities, the margin out of the sale of surplus is much lower than the previous group.

Higher margin which is the greatest incentive for higher marketed surplus is also determined by the marketing cost. Marketing cost which includes the cost of transportation, commission to middlemen, weights, measures, handling and other expenses can be reduced when the surplus is sold in a bulk rather than in a small quantity. Strong bargaining power may also reduce such costs. It is revealed from our study that Rs. 6.54 is the average marketing cost in the Valley. The first two categories of farmers pay Rs. 12.35 and Rs. 8.23 respectively per quintal as marketing cost. This is much higher than the average, mainly due to the reasons discussed above whereas the other two categories of farmers pay Rs. 5.54 and Rs. 5.59 per quintal as marketing expenses. It once again needs to be reiterated that the third category of farmers incur the lowest amount of marketing cost enabling them to reach the highest margin as well. This once again supports our evidence to the fact that this group of farmers manages their marketing strategy of their surplus in the most effective and efficient manner. The farmers of largest size holdings have greater potentiality for earning a higher level of margin and generating more surpluses, but often fail to do so

The farmers belonging to the third size holding could have increased their margin and hence also their surplus even further, if they had sold a greater proportion of their surplus directly in the market rather than going through middlemen. However when a large volume of the surplus has to be sold middlemen will have to be relied upon as it is not possible for the farmers themselves to sell directly in the market as in the case of small and marginal farmers, who are able to do so due to the small quantity of produce sold by them. It is for this reason that our survey reveals that the proportion of farmers disposing off their surplus through middlemen increases in direct proportion to the size of land holdings. Only 28.74 per cent farmers among the small size-holdings sell their surplus through middlemen, while almost the entire proportion of the farmers of large size-holdings being as high as almost 92 per cent depend on the middlemen. It is therefore evident that middlemen play a very important role in the marketing scenario of Barak Valley of South Assam. The farmers, particularly the ones belonging to large holdings are totally dependent on them for disposing off their surplus.

Dependence of small and marginal farmers is less on the middlemen, since our survey reveals that 41.38 per cent of the farmers themselves among this group sell the products directly in the market being the highest among all the groups. In contrast, only 13.33 per cent of the farmers among large size-holdings sell directly in the market. The percentage of such farmers decrease in direct proportion to the size of land holdings. It is therefore revealed from our analysis that, lower the dependence on the middlemen, higher the sale of paddy in the market by the farmers themselves and higher the dependence on the middlemen, lower the direct sale of paddy by the farmers themselves.

Therefore in Barak Valley where facilities are extremely limited and undeveloped, reliance on the middlemen increases, especially when a large amount as in the case of large size holdings have to be sold. Though middlemen absorb much of the profit that could have gone to the large farms, yet middlemen are indispensable in the market scenario of paddy. On average, middlemen in India appropriate upto 48 per cent of the price paid by consumers for paddy. The Government therefore with the intention of safeguarding the interest of both producers as well as the consumers, has specified some certified Government dealers and stockists. In Barak Valley, middlemen have an additional role in the disposal of marketed surplus which arises mainly due to the extremely poor road condition and communication system. Left on their own, farmers may never be able to bring the produce themselves to the market and if they are expected to undertake this task, marketing costs will increase even further. This may not only reduce their margins, but a part of the burden may be passed on to the consumers, who may therefore have to pay a much higher price. In the process both producers and consumers would be the losers.

The distance from the place of production to the marketing place is revealed in Table 4.8, which shows that this distance increases along with increase in land holdings. The distance is the lowest of only 3 km for small farmers and about 4 km for the largest size holdings. Such a possibility may arise since large land holdings spread over a wider area are often located in the interiors and are rarely near the commercial centers. This factor may be another reason behind increasing dependence of large farmers on the middlemen in comparison to small farmers.

The dominant role of middlemen which may be expected to continue in the future also therefore needs to be regulated, though it may not be done totally. Regular information relating to the market price and their change is an important determinant of the generation of sufficient quantum of marketed surplus. Inadequate information may lead to the disposition of the product at a time when prices are low. This lowers the extent of margin, lowering in turn the desire and the interest to generate sufficient quantum of marketed surplus. Table 4.8 also reveals that the awareness about the prevalent market price is the least among the farmers of small holdings. The percentage of farmers aware of the market price, among this group is only 29 per cent increasing to 36 per cent among the next size holding. The awareness level rises sharply to 67 and 75 per cent respectively for the next two groups. Though the awareness level do not have any direct relationship with variation of marketed surplus according to size-holdings, but it certainly compels the small size-holders to dispose off their produce even at the most unfavourable price. It may therefore transpire that inadequate knowledge and lower level of awareness among farmers of this group may be an important consideration for the generation of marketed surplus. It is mostly due to this reason that the margin through the sale of paddy which is one of the most crucial determinants of marketed surplus is negative for the lower two size holdings, but experiences a positive value for the bigger size holdings in whose case the level of awareness too rises suddenly. In fact, the margin per quintal and per hectare is negative for the lowest size holding to the extent of Rs. 107 and Rs. 5216 respectively. The margin continues to be negative though diminishes substantially for the next size holding to Rs. 32.48 and Rs. 250 respectively. Negative margin becomes positive for the next two size holdings. It is respectively Rs. 97.47 and 12.17 per quintal and Rs. 4180 and Rs. 4329 per hectare for holdings of 2.01-3.0 and above hectare. The margin per quintal not of the highest but the third category of land holding that emerges to be recording the best performance reveal that they conduct production and sale on a commercial basis and not merely for the sake of sustenance as in the case of the previous two groups. Such is not the experience of farmers of large size holdings whose profit per hectare though the highest, but profit per quintal is below their counterpart in the previous category. The reason could perhaps be that they depend mostly on middlemen who may be appropriating a major share of the margin. It can also be that since a major chunk of their income comes from non-agricultural sources, they themselves do not take much interest in raising efficiency in production and sale and are characterized by behaviourial attitude which is complacen in nature. Our data reveals that the percentage of income earned from non-agricultural sources is as high as 34.35 per cent for the highest land holding and as low as only 12.07 per cent for smallest holding sizes. Consequently, raising the level of profit or generating the optimum quantum of marketed surplus may not be their areas of priority.

However, examination of margin per household reveals that this margin is the highest among the largest size holdings and lowest among the smallest size holdings. This may be purely due to the fact that number of household with large size holdings is smaller whereas a large number of the cultivators belong to the small size groups.

It is therefore revealed that the farmers belonging to the first two categories of land holdings indulge in distress sale like the farmers of any other poor agricultural state. Since cash requirement is the major priority, they neither bother about the time of sale of their produce or the highest price which their produce might have fetched. It may be due to this reason that the expected price at which they would like to sell their produce is only Rs. 628 for the lowest groups and increases steadily along with size of holdings to Rs. 708 for the highest group. Since immediate cash in hand, soon after the harvesting period is not an urgent requirement of the rich farmers, it is not only that their price expectation is higher, but they are even willing and can actually afford to wait for the price to be favourable to them, which is normally the case during the lean season. It is therefore evident as in the discussion earlier, that the highest proportion of the farmers belonging to the small size holdings dispose off their produce immediately following the harvesting season, whereas the highest proportion of the farmers with higher land holdings dispose off their produce during the lean season. Experience of distress sale is also evident from Table 4.3, where we find that the highest quantum of purchase of 545 quintals is undertaken by the farmers of lowest size holdings, which increases steadily to 289, 29 and only 26 quintals for the largest size holdings. Considering the percentage of purchase of paddy from the market, for the same reasons, 24.05 and 12.34 per cent of small farmers purchase from the market as against only 1.93 per cent and 1.58 per cent respectively of farmers belonging to the larger two groups, as is evident from Table 4.3 above. Inspite of such large quantum of purchase from the market the smallest size holdings still manages to generate small quantum of surplus to the extent of 0.52 per cent (Table

4.5) of the total output. This is in sharp contrast to the behavioural pattern of small farmers in other parts of the country where they are hardly able to generate a surplus, though they have been engaged in production over the years. They are caught in such a vicious circle of poverty, through debts, inefficient production and low productivity that they are not able to extricate themselves out of it. Considering such grim reality farmers of Barak Valley however poor, have the desire to generate a small proportion of their output as marketed surplus, notwithstanding the large quantum of purchase for self consumption from the market as well as consuming a large proportion of the production themselves.

4.7 Borrowings and Debts as a Determinant of Marketed Surplus

What therefore transpires from the analysis of the data and discussion above is that the extent of poverty is a crucial determinant of marketed surplus. In fact, all the pivotal factors that lead to the generation of marketed surplus are the outcome of the economic status of the farmers directly or indirectly. It is therefore pertinent to also examine the extent, nature and sources of borrowing of the farmers of the different land holdings, which may convey some idea relating to the desire, ability as well as the efforts made to conduct agriculture on commercial lines.

Table 4.9: Credit Facilities to Farmers and Marketed Surplus

Size Holding	*0-1 hect.*	*1.01-2.0 hect.*	*2.01-3.0 hect.*	*3.01 hect. and above*
P.C. of farmers who borrow for production	35.63	33.69	31.15	28.33
P.C. of farmers who borrow from banks	2.29	9.78	11.48	21.66
P.C. of farmers borrowing from money-lenders	33.33	23.91	19.67	6.66

Source: Based on Field Survey.

Table 4.9 above clearly reveals that the proportion of farmers borrowing clearly declines along with a rise in size holdings. The percentage of farmers who are in debt is as high as 35.63 per cent among the smallest size holdings, declining steadily to 33.69 per cent, 31.15 per cent and 28.33 per cent according to holding size. It is only natural that due to more financial crisis, borrowing is highest among small farmers and least among the rich farmers. However, what are relevant for our purposes are the sources of borrowing. Among the small farmers as high as 33.33 per cent borrow from the money-lenders and only 6.66 per cent farmers belonging to large size-holdings borrow from similar sources, only for the purpose of production. Other studies (Sengupta, 2005) have also shown similar trend of larger borrowing among small farmers from money- lenders due to easy accessibility and less procedural formalities. However, what is of concern to us from the point of view of marketed surplus is the fact that, the burden of paying off huge sums as interest payments, compels them to sell off their produce at a unfavourable time and unfavourable price. Payment is made to such village money-lenders in terms of kind instead of cash, reducing to that extent the quantum of the surplus. If such financial pressures and obligations could have been avoided, perhaps it could have encouraged to conducting the business of marketing on more scientific lines and on systematic and methodical basis. Such efforts might have led to increasing the quantum of surplus. For just the opposite reasons, the relatively stronger financial positions of big farmers and smaller proportion of their borrowings from banks, where 21.66 per cent of the farmers avail of bank credit, enables them to conduct production and marketing on more systematic lines. They are not under constant pressure of paying high interest to banks as their counterparts in small size holdings. This enables them to concentrate more on the actual business of marketing, and thereby contribute more to the generation of marketed surplus.

The discussion above not only draws the broad contours of marketed surplus according to size holdings in this Valley of South Assam, but also enables us to identify the most crucial determinants of marketed surplus. However, to know the relative weightage of these determinants, we shall fit them into the models of the study in the subsequent chapters.

The amount of marketed surplus generated may also be governed by the overall financial strength of the farmers. The overall financial strength is determined by the total income of the farmers both from agricultural as well as from non-agricultural sources, as well as the saving that they are able to generate, which in turn determines the ability for capital formation.

Table 4.10: Marketable Surplus and Various Source of Income of the Farmers

Size Holding	*0-1 hect.*	*1.01-2.0 hect.*	*2.01-3.0 hect.*	*3.01 hect. and above*	*Total*
P.C. of farmers producing other crops along with paddy	11.49	21.74	24.59	36.66	22.33
P.C. of income from agricultural sources	18.35	17-21	42.99	44.02	33.85
P.C. of income from non-agricultural sources	12.07	18.90	35.68	34.35	100
P.C. of income saved by the farmers	—	05.15	44.08	58.82	45.66
P.C. of income spent on consumption	97.27	70.21	48.31	33.21	—

Source: Estimated from Field Survey Data.

Table 4.10 above reveals the percentage of income of the farmers of different size holdings, both from agricultural as well as non-agricultural sources. It also focuses attention to the farmers who do not depend entirely on sale of paddy as their sole source of agricultural income, but extend their cultivation activities to other crops as well. Among the other sources of agricultural income in Barak Valley is mainly the income derived from the sale of arecanuts, which occupies an important place in the total commercial transaction of the farmers. The table also draws attention to income from sources other than from agriculture. This may indicate the extent to which the farmers actually want to conduct agriculture on a commercial basis and indicates their desire to increase the quantum of marketed surplus. Apart from that, the table also reveals the amount of total income which the farmers of the various land holdings are able to save. This will throw an important light on the financial strength of the farmers, which has tremendous implications, both for capital formation in agricultural sector as well as future trend for the generation of marketed surplus.

It is further revealed that in the entire valley only about 22.23 per cent of the farmers are engaged in the production of crops other than paddy, revealing that paddy is the main crop that is cultivated in the region. It also reveals the total dependence of the farmers on this major crop since the agro climatic features of the region do not permit the production of any other crop which may be commercially viable.

Examination of the percentage of farmers according to size of land holdings who engage themselves in the production of other crops show that the proportion increases linearly with size of land holdings. In other words, it implies that farmers with small land holdings are more dependent totally on paddy. As their economic condition improves the size of their landholding also increases and they are consequently able to devote as well as able to take risk in investing time, labour and money for the cultivation of other crops. This may also indicate that their ability to spread to other crops enables them to have greater control over the release of marketed surplus of paddy. Such farmers are able to hold back stock when prices are low and release them only when prices are high and remunerative. This they are able to do much better than their counterparts with small holding size, because they are totally dependent for their main source of income only on one crop, weakening their bargaining position and their holding capacity of marketed surplus of paddy. We therefore find that only 11.49 per cent of farmers with the smallest size holdings devote to the cultivation of other crops. The percentage rises to 21.74 to 24.59 and finally to 36.66 per cent for the highest land holdings. It thus implies that the financial strength of the farmers is an important consideration for the generation of marketed surplus. Extreme poverty of the farmers, belonging to the smaller holding size is evident from the fact that though cultivation is their main occupation and the major crop they cultivate is paddy, yet the income which they earn from agriculture is a meagre 18.75 per cent and 17 per cent respectively of their total income. This is an indication of the fact that though they devote most of their time, land, labour and all other efforts for paddy cultivation, yet because they are forced to dispose off their surplus at an unfavourable time and place, they do not get the highest return. Consequently, the amount of income that they desire from the sale of marketed surplus is the lowest among all their counterparts. The farmers supplement their family income by working mostly as wage labourers with big farmers and engages themselve in all other types of odd jobs, including working as daily labourers. Some of them also engage themselves in small trade and business in their own villages. All these activities are undertaken with the sole purpose of supplementing family income, though they consider agriculture as their main occupation.

It needs to be noted that the situation changes when income from other sources is examined in case of farmers belonging to larger holding sizes. A sudden rise is recorded in the proportion of such income in case of these two groups which are 43 and 44 per cent respectively. For the third and fourth category of land holdings this may be a reflection of not only the fact that agriculture is their major occupation, but more importantly, that due to many factors, such as greater degree of awareness relating to the right price and greater financial ability, storage capacity and thereby greater capacity to increase production, their bargaining position over the sale of marketable surplus is much higher. They have considerable amount of say over the time and place as well as the price at which surplus is to be sold. This is also evident from our earlier discussion, where we have seen that the price at which the holders of the two larger size land holdings sell the product is higher than the price at which smaller farmers sell their product. It was also discussed earlier that such farmers do not sell the major portion of their produce during the immediate post harvest season but sell the surplus during the lean season. All these experiences allow them to seek a higher price, enabling them to increase the share of their income from agricultural sector. Coupled with this is also the fact that the volume of their production is much higher than in comparison to other farmers. Another feature associated with these farmers is that, considerable financial strength enables them to divert their business to other areas of agriculture over and above paddy cultivation. Production and trade in arecanut, which is one of the most important product of the region and fetches a highly remunerative price is undertaken by these farmers. Consequently, this also adds to their total income.

However, it is also observed from the Table 4.10 above, that the proportion of income from non-agricultural sources is much higher in case of farmers belonging to large size-holdings, once again adding strength to their financial capability. Farmers belonging to the largest size holdings of both sizes have around 34 per cent of income from non agricultural sources. In contrast, the proportion is only 12.?7 and 18.97 per cent respectively for the lower two classes. This may indeed sound paradoxical because big farmers have a high proportion of income both from agriculture as well as from non-agricultural sources. The reason for this explanation is sought in the fact that due to higher level of education, particularly higher education among the family members of large size holdings, employment in sectors outside agriculture is quite common. However, the same experience is not true in case of other farmers. In fact, most of the farmers of large size-holdings do not cultivate the land themselves, but get it done by hired labourers or cultivators, unlike the poor farmers who cultivate their own land themselves. As a result all the family members of poor farmers are engaged in agriculture and do not have enough time or scope to engage in other full time jobs, except during lean seasons. In contrast, in case of farmers of large size holdings, with the exception of a few family members who are mostly engaged in supervision of their land and matters relating to the sale of surplus, the other members of the family mostly migrate to other places and engage themselves in service or secondary sectors. It is due to this that their income from non-agricultural sources is higher. All these factors, lead to further strengthening the financial position of such farmers.

The evidence relating to the financial strength of the farmers belonging to various categories of land holdings is also supported by the percentage of income that is saved by this category of farmers. It is therefore not at all surprising that the weak financial base as evidenced by the small quantum of marketed surplus, low income, distress sale of the farmers of small land holdings at unfavourable prices and repurchase from the market at a higher prices for their own consumption, high level of indebtedness, particularly the greater level of dependence on money-lenders, cannot expect to generate any savings. In fact, such small and marginal farmers are mostly steeped in debts. There is therefore absolute absence of any type of reinvestment either for the purpose of regular production or long term capital investment. Along with increase in holding size, there is also a commensurate increase of marketed surplus and therefore, evidence from our earlier analysis also suggest that there is a steady rise in almost all the variables governing their financial capacity. The result of this is that the proportion of income saved also reveals a rising trend with the second category of land holding recording 5.15 per cent saving followed by 44.08 per cent and 58.82 per cent respectively recorded by the next category of farmers. The well off farmers save almost 60 per cent of their income. This is only too clear when we observe that small farmers spent almost 97 per cent of their income on consumption. This leaves them with hardly any substantial amount to be invested for the sake of agriculture, which is their main occupation and the main source of their income. As expected, the percentage of income used for consumption requirement declines steadily along with a rise in income increasing the ability to save and the ability to reinvest the savings for the purpose of capital formation in the agricultural sector. It is therefore not surprising, that the percentage of farmers using better technologies requiring more investment rises steadily along with size holdings. Such experiences therefore have direct bearing on the volume of marketed surplus generated in the Valley.

4.8 Conclusion

What therefore, transpires from the above discussion is that there are several factors, such as retention, price level in the market, margin, extent of awareness, time of sale of the produce, all of which in combination determines the generation of marketed surplus in the Valley. Most of these behavioural traits of marketed surplus though almost similar to that of the other parts of the country, yet in this part of the country one significant feature that needs to be emphasized is that though small and marginal farmers indulge in forced sales and resort to repurchase of paddy from the market, yet there is no evidence of negative marketed surplus among such farmers as in other parts of the country. This is inspite of the fact that such farmers are characterized by poverty and subsistence level of farming.

References

Agarwal A.L. (1970): "Marketed Agricultural Surpluses in Relation to Size of Land Holdings—A Case Study (UP)" *Agricultural Situation in India,* Volume 25.

Agarwal N.L. (1986): "Agricultural Prices and Marketing in India", Mittal Publication, New Delhi.

Bhargava, P.N. and Rastogi V.S. (1972): "Study of Marketable Surplus of Paddy in Burdwan District", *Indian Journal of Agricultural Economics,* Volume 27.

Bardhan, Pranab and Kalpana, Bardhan (1969): "The Problem of Marketed Surplus of Cereals", *Economic and Political Weekly,* Volume IV, No. 26 and 29.

Dandekar, V. M. (1964): "Prices, Production and Marketed Surplus of Foodgrains", *Indian Journal of Agricultural Economics,* Vol. 19.

Gangwar, A.C. and Goel, R.C. (1980): "Impact of Green Revolution on Marketing costs and Margins of rice in Haryana", *Agricultural Marketing,* Volume 22.

Ghosh, Deepak (1987): "A Theoretical Model of Behaviour of Marketed Surplus in a Partially Monetised Economy", *The Indian Economic Journal,* Volume 34.

Goswami, P.C. and P.D. Saikia (1968): "Disposals of Paddy by Surplus Growers—A study of Assam", *Economic and Political Weekly,* Volume 3.

Gupta, G.S. (1980): "Agricultural Price Policy and Farm Incomes" *Economic and Political Weekly,* Volume XV.

Jakhade, V.M. and Mazumdar, N.A. (1964): "Response of Agricultural Producers to Prices—The Case of Jute and Rice in India", *Indian Journal of Agricultural Economics,* Volume 19.

Kahloon, A.S. and Dwivedi, H.N. (1963): "Interrelationship between Production and Marketable Surplus", *Assam Economic Review.*

Kahloon, A.S. and Reed, C.E. (1961): "Problems of Marketable Surplus in Indian Agriculture", *Indian Journal of Agricultural Economics,* Vol. 16.

Kaul, J.L. and D.S. Siddhu (1971): "Acreage Response to Prices for

Major Crops in Punjab—An Econometric Study" *Indian Journal of Agricultural Economics*, Volume 26.

Lakshmanan, P.P. (1967): "Transport of Paddy from the Farms to the Markets in India", *Agricultural Situation in India*, Volume XXII, No. 3.

Naqvi, S. (1961): "Problems of Marketable Surplus in Indian Agriculture", *Indian Journal of Agricultural Economics*, Volume 16.

Natarajan, B. (1961): "Problems of Marketable Surplus in Indian Agriculture", *Indian Journal of Agricultural Economics*, Volume 16.

Peraskar, P.K. and Subba, B.V. (1984): 'Production and Marketed Surplus of Rice in the Deltas of South" *Agricultural Situation in India*, Volume 21.

Prasad, J. (1989): "Marketable Surplus and Market Performance", Mittal Publications, Delhi.

Rao, P.V.G.K. (1965): "Marketed Surplus and Agricultural Production—A Case Study of a Village in UP", *Agricultural Situation in India*, Volume 20.

Rudra, A. (1973): "Marketing Behaviour of Big, Medium and Small Farms", *Economic and Political Weekly*, Volume II, No. 27.

Sharma, P.P. (1969): "Marketable Surplus in Subsistence: A Case Study of a District Village in Rajasthan", *Economic and Political Weekly*, Volume 4.

Shastri, C.P. (1963): "Interrelationship between Production, Prices and Marketable Surplus in Bihar", *Agricultural Situation in India*, Volume 18.

Sengupta, K. (1998): "Behavioural Pattern of Marketable Surplus in Barak Valley of South Assam", *Agricultural Situation in India*, GoI, New Delhi.

Vyas, V.S. (1966): "Factors Affecting Marketable Surplus and Marketed Supplies—A Case Study of the Region in Gujarat and Rajasthan", *Artha Vikas*, Volume 2.

5

Determinants of Marketed Surplus: An Empirical Analysis

5.1 Introduction

In the analysis so far we have identified some of the crucial factors that determine the behaviourial pattern of marketed surplus in the Valley in general as well as size holdings of farmers. However to determine the relative weights of the various factors, we shall adapt some models, the results of which shall be discussed in the present chapter. Such an analysis will reveal the nature and extent of the relationship between marketed surplus and other factors and highlight the reasons for the behaviourial pattern of marketed surplus in the Valley.

It is a common experience in general that no single factor effects the behaviourial pattern of marketed surplus and no single factor is equally important at all times and at all places. Even in the same place no single factor can be equally significant for all holding sizes. Further some factors may be operating simultaneously in some places, whereas in others one or two factors may be important. In the foregoing analysis we have seen that marketed surplus increases linearly with respect to size holdings. Some of the crucial factors identified so far in the study is retention. However, this may not be true for all categories of land holdings.

Among the various components of retention the study reveals that different components of retention is significant for different size holdings. For instance, retention for consumption is dominant for some while retention for wage payments, seeds or for purposes of future sale appears to be important for the rest. Production is a definite factor determining marketed surplus not only in this region, but for all other places too. However, whether production plays the same role for various categories of holding sizes is yet to be known.

One of the most important determinants of marketable surplus is the price of the paddy that farmers get from the sale of his product. Remunerative prices enlarges the size of the marketed surplus, though its impact on farmers of different size holdings do certainly vary. The time and disposal of marketed surplus is another crucial factor that determines the volume of the surplus. Therefore in an attempt to capture the essence of the weightage of these various determinants of marketed surplus we shall specify a few models which we shall test to further strengthen and support our earlier findings.

5.2 Empirical Analysis of the Determinants of Marketed Surplus

In a region dominated by poor farmers, retention normally appears to be a crucial factor of marketed surplus. Consumption is the most important determinant of retention. This is more true for those places where the product considered is also the staple food of the farmers. Small and marginal farmers due to their limited output, retain a higher proportion of their production for the purpose of consumption, whereas opposite is the case with respect to the rich farmers, who retain a major portion of the produce for the purpose of the future to be used as seeds, for consumption as well as for future sales when prices are much higher. Retention is also made for the purpose of payments in kind for wages, credit as well as for land taken on hire, which differs from farmer to farmer with various size holdings. It is therefore pertinent that to capture the relative weightage of retention and its various components as determinants of marketed surplus, we have used net instead of gross marketed surplus, because the net value would give us the idea relating to the exact quantum of the produce that would be actually offered for sale in the market, as against the marketed surplus in general, because that would include repurchase from the market and may therefore fail to reveal the true quantum of market disposal.

In the model it is hypothesized that net marketed surplus is a negative function of retention. In other words whenever there is an increase in the components of retention there would be a decline in marketed surplus and vice versa. In an attempt to measure the relative weightage of retention we adopt the following model, which is as follows:

$$\text{NMS} = a - b\text{Rtsd} - c\text{Rtsale} - d\text{Rtfc} + \text{Ui} \qquad \ldots(1)$$

where

Rtsd = retention for seeds
Rtsale = retention for sale
Rtfc = retention for future consumption.
Ui = the disturbance term

Though retention is also undertaken for the purpose of payments in kind for wages as well as credit and to landlords for taking land on hire, yet most farmers particularly the small and the marginal ones are unable to specify the exact amount of retention separately for each of these items. Nor is there any fixed quantity used separately for these various forms of payments. We have therefore retained the components of retention only for the purpose of seeds, consumption and future sales.

The models mentioned above have first been tested for Barak Valley of south Assam as a whole and in the next section they have been tested for the small and large holding sizes separately. This has been done to examine whether the behavioural patterns of all the farmers conform to the general pattern or whether there is a divergence in their behavioural pattern depending upon the size of their land holdings.

From our earlier analysis we have seen that retention is an important factor determining the generation of marketed surplus. In fact, higher the quantum of retention lower is the volume of net marketed surplus. Therefore any attempt at increasing marketed surplus in the Valley may be undertaken by reducing the quantum of retention. This may be done by going in for increased monetization of the remote and interior sectors of the economy A considerable portion of the transaction in rural areas is still done through direct exchange of paddy with essential items of consumption by the farmers and is therefore not accounted as marketed surplus. Such payments are made in terms of the product produced, particularly when it is a staple food like paddy, for the purpose of wage payments, repayment of credit and payments to landlords for leasing in lands. This results in reducing the quantum of marketed surplus. Though conversion to monetization is possible in terms of monetary payments for the above items, and thereby reduce the quantum of retention, it is more difficult to reduce retention which is undertaken for the purposes of consumption by the farmers themselves along with their family members, amount that is retained for future sales and the amount that is kept back to be used as seeds for the next harvesting season.

For purposes of policy formulations, it is extremely important to know the behavioural pattern of retention according to holding size. For this purpose we have tested the model for the lower holding size consisting of the first two size holdings and for the higher holding sizes. The results of the models for both the holding sizes are reported below:

Small Holding Size:

$$NMS = -128.456 + 1.244\ Ret + Ui \quad R^2 = .755;\ F = 12.296$$
$$(-1.247) \quad (3.507)$$

Large Holding Size:

$$NMS = 354.342 - .824\ Ret + Ui \quad R^2 = .540;\ F = 4.699$$
$$(1.113) \quad (-2.168)$$

The function is acceptable for big size holdings. The function explains 54 per cent of the relationship. However, the function is not acceptable for the small and marginal farmers, since though the value of R^2 is high and the coefficient too is significant, yet it cannot be accepted on theoretical grounds. This implies that retention power is simply non-existent among the small farmers. For farmers of such category cash is the first requirement. They require cash not for the purpose of increasing agricultural production but either to meet their daily requirements or to repay the debts of the money lenders. Debts are incurred mostly for unproductive, non remunerative purposes. In contrast, farmers of large size holdings require cash mostly for productive purposes, especially when they are able to depend for the purchase of their consumption items from non-agricultural sources of income. Their retention capacity is much stronger also in comparison to the small farmers. Higher retention power among them also reveal that they are guided more by speculative and precautionary motives, which are conspicuous by their absence among the small and marginal farmers, since subsistence is their sole motive.

In an attempt to test the second model and identify the relative weightage of the various components of retention we have next tested the model the result of which are reported below:

$$NMS = a - b\ Rt\ sd + c\ Rt\ Sale - d\ Rtf\ c + Ui \qquad \ldots(2)$$

$$NMS = 854.551 - 23.271 \text{ Rt sd} + 1.950 \text{ Rt sale} - 653 \text{ Rt fc}$$
$$(2.829) \quad (-.988) \qquad (2.950) \qquad (-.151)$$
$$R^2 = .558; F = 3.364$$

The value of R^2 in comparison to the first model is reduced to .56, reducing thereby the explanatory power of the variable also. The coefficient of the variables of retention for seed and future consumption though possesing the requisite signs, are not statistically significant. Hence they are not accepted for our purpose. The coefficient of retention for future sale though appears to be statistically significant cannot be accepted for our purpose for theoretical reasons, as the coefficient posses the positive sign. Due to all these reasons the above model cannot be accepted, though the first model where total retention is taken as an explanatory variable is accepted for our purpose.

Among all the components of retention, consumption, particularly among the small and marginal farmers all over the country has always been the most important reason for determining marketed surplus, we have therefore specified another model, in which we have taken consumption of paddy by the farmers as the explanatory variable. The model adopted for this purpose is as follows.

$$NMS = a - bRt \text{ cosump} + Ui \qquad ..(3)$$

The estimated results of the model is as follows:

$$NMS = -15.838 + 1.032 \text{ Rt cosump} + Ui$$
$$(-.022) \quad (.801)$$
$$R^2 = .060; F = .641$$

The results reveal that the model cannot be accepted either on theoretical or statistical grounds and the explanatory power of the variable too is extremely weak as revealed by the value of R^2. For all size holdings considered together, retention for self consumption does not appear to be significant determinant factor of marketed surplus in this valley. However, break up of the results according to holding size may depict a different picture, since in most places, particularly the ones dominated by small and marginal farmers, retention for consumption always occupy a significant proportion of total retention and it had always been an important determinant of marketed surplus. The results of this above model according to holding size may therefore provide an indepth knowledge of this explanatory variable.

The results of consumption as an explanatory variable according to holding size is reported below:

Small Size Holding:

$$NMS = 33.90 + .321 \text{ Consump} + Ui$$
$$(.872)$$

R^2 .166; F = .795

Large Size Holding:

$$NMS = 333.452 - 1.54 \text{ Consump} + Ui$$
$$(2.842)$$

R^2 .669: F =8.078

The results of the model for the two category of land holdings reveal that the function is not acceptable for the lower income group, both because the explanatory power of the variable is weak and also because the coefficient of the independent variable is insignificant. However the function is acceptable for large size holdings.

The function explains almost 67 per cent of the relationship and the coefficient of the independent variable too is significant. The results of the function though initially may appear to be surprising, may not really be so, since it implies that poor farmers do not have the capacity to hold back any substantial quantity of paddy even for the purpose of self consumption and are compelled to go in for immediate sale of their produce in the immediate post harvest season, since they are in urgent need of cash. As a result retention for the purpose of consumption does not have any significant impact on the quantum of marketed surplus offered by them. Such findings are substantiated by our earlier findings in the previous chapter. For the purpose of their own consumption they are forced to buy at a later period at a much higher price. Consequently, self consumption, does not appear to be of any significance as far as the determinant factor of marketed surplus is concerned. The same, however, is not true in case of large size holdings, because rich farmers do not indulge in any substantial amount of repurchase from the market. Such farmers retain almost the entire proportion of their consumption from their total production for the purpose of self consumption. Consequently, consumption by this section of the farmers appear to be having significant impact on the quantum of marketed surplus.

According to the tabular analysis it was revealed that smaller farmers consume more than the large farmers and a greater percentage of their production is therefore devoted for the purpose of consumption. The break up of the regression model, according to land holdings reveals the underlying truth, because it reveals that though the consumption of the small cultivators may be more a major proportion of that is actually repurchased from the market and not retained from their own production. This is only too evident when we also examine the quantity of purchase of paddy from the market, both by the rich as well as by the poor farmers. In the absence of regression model such findings would not have come out clearly.

It is therefore a matter of serious concern that even today there are a large number of farmers who do not have the capacity for retention, even for the purpose of their own consumption. Resorting to "distress sale" by this group as was maintained by Dharam Narain from data of almost 50 years earlier, relating to the period 1950-51 is prevalent even today. He calls it a source of embarrassing income effect with respect to marketed surplus—has continued over time (Raj, Sen, Rao 1988) On the basis of the market arrival since 1961-62 it was shown and argued in the study that over time marketed surplus has actually declined, indicating that powerful income effects were at work, either by way of increased per capita consumption of foodgrains by the farming community or the increase in the farmer's capacity for retention. Since the present work is based on the cross analysis of data and not a time series one, we are not in a position to make comment on the trend of marketed surplus and retention over time among the farmers of Barak Valley.

It might therefore be concluded that for owners of small size holdings, more than consumption some other factors, such as price incentive or the return from the sale of their produce, or any other kind of monetary benefit may be assuming greater weightage. This could be quite possible since due to poverty cash requirement is their main consideration. Therefore before we specify some more models in an attempt to identify the determinants of marketed surplus according to land size, we use price incentive as the determinant fact or of marketed surplus.

Price incentive as discussed in the earlier analysis is the most important factor determining the desire to generate the requisite quantum of marketed surplus. Higher the market price of paddy, greater is the desire to offer more for sale, which may be even at the cost of lower volume of retention. When prices are higher, during lean season, there is a greater desire to offer more for sale. Consequently, marketed surplus rises in comparison to a situation when prices are lower during post harvest season. There in an attempt to examine how farmers belonging to different size holdings respond to price at a given point of time for which we specify the next model stated below.

$$NMS = a + b\, Pr + Ui \qquad \ldots(4)$$

where Pr = price of paddy

The relationship is hypothesized as positive implying that higher price means higher volume of marketed surplus, exceptional cases notwithstanding.

The results of the estimated equation mentioned above is as follows:

$$NMS = -4010.037 + 8.776\, Pr + Ui$$
$$(-1.829) \quad (2.088)$$

$$R^2 = .304;\ F = 4.361$$

The above function cannot be accepted as the value of R^2 is only.304 and is also insignificant, though coefficient of the independent variable is significant and possesses the expected sign also. In view of the fact that price provides the highest incentive for the generation of marketed surplus, the non acceptability of the above function, induces us to test the model according to different size holdings. This will enable us to know exactly how farmers of different holding size respond to price changes. This is because small and marginal farmers, though requiring cash, are unable to offer more as marketed surplus, since they neither have the holding capacity due to inadequate storage facilities or due to their urgency of immediate cash. Consequently, experience suggests that even at lower or unrumenerative prices they offer more as marketed surplus than their counterparts of large sized holdings. As a result when we take the overall estimated result for the Valley as a whole, it emerges as though price is not a significant determinant factor of marketed surplus. Therefore here too examination of the result of the model according to holding size may reveal the exact quantitative relationship of the variables.

The estimation of the above function according to holding size reveal the following results stated below:

Size Holdings:

$$NMS = 3587.179 + 7.634\ Pr + Ui \qquad R^2 = .657;\ F = 7.652$$
$$(-2.632) \qquad (2.766)$$

Large Size Holdings:

$$NMS = 10239.29 - 16.968\ Pr + Ui \qquad R^2 = .307;\ F = 1.772$$
$$(1.465) \qquad (-1.331)$$

Contrary to our expectation, it is revealed that the function though acceptable for small farmers cannot be expected to be equally relevant for the large farmers, as R^2 is only .307 and the insignificance of the coefficient and the change of its sign do not permit us to accept the function for large size holdings. In contrast it is revealed that almost 66 per cent of the relationship is explained by this function for the small farmers and the coefficient possess the satisfactory value and is also statistically significant. This implies that monetary incentive is the most important incentive for the poor farmers. Cash requirement is the most important priority for such farmers, even more than the necessity of their own consumption requirement. In contrast, price does not appear to be an important determinant factor for rich farmers. This implies that agriculture is not conducted on commercial basis perhaps because income from agricultural sources may not be the sole source of earning unlike as in the case of small and marginal farmers. Consequently, production appears to be the most important determining factor of marketed surplus in the Valley revealing a positive and linear relationship with marketed surplus.

Marketed surplus therefore is a positive function of price for the poor farmers, unlike the findings of Dharam Narain according to whom marketed surplus is a negative function of price for all categories of farmers taken together. It needs to be mentioned further that negative sign before the constant for the small farmers imply that whatever may be the price, repurchase of foodgrains is bound to dominate the small and marginal farmers, though the same may not be true for the large farmers.

In an attempt to capture the influence of the above variables jointly on NMS, the next model that we have adopted is as follows:

$$NMS = a + b\ Consp + c\ Prod + d\ Ret + Ui \qquad \ldots(5)$$

The estimated result of the function is as follows:

$$NMS = -98.746 - .206\ Consp + .306\ Prod + .345\ Ret$$
$$(.0123)\quad (.786)\qquad\qquad (.546)$$
$$R^2 = .794;\ F = 10.21$$

In the above estimated equation though R^2 is almost as high as .80, yet the function cannot be accepted for our purpose, as none of the coefficients of the independent variables is significant and the coefficient of retention has also changed its sign, indicating the presence of multi collinearity. Multi collinearity is not surprising since there is a close relationship among the variables, such as retention for future production and the level of consumption. The function therefore cannot be accepted for our purpose.

The next model that we shall specify will also be multiple regression model, in which in addition to the independent variables adopted in the earlier model, price is also added as an additional independent variable. The model would therefore take the following form:

$$NMS = a + b\ Consp + c\ Prod + d\ Ret + e\ Pr + Ui \qquad \ldots(7)$$

The result of the estimated equation is as follows:

$$NMS = -.3099.092 + .175\ Consp + .363\ Prod - 3.7\ Ret + 5.393\ Pr$$
$$(.233) \quad (2.027) \quad (-.74) \quad (91.841)$$
$$R^2 = .861;\ F = 10.866$$

Like the earlier equation this equation too cannot be accepted, though R^2 is as high as .861. The reason for this is that most of the coefficients with the exception of the production coefficient are statistically insignificant, though most of them have the required signs. As a result none of the above two models can be accepted for our purpose.

Directly linked up with the issue of price obtained by the sale of marketed surplus is also the interrelated issue of the margin that is obtained by the sale of paddy. In fact, the extent of margin obtained by the farmers play a more crucial role in comparison to even the price of paddy. Higher price of paddy with a lower margin may not be of much help to the farmers. Margin is defined as the cost minus the cost of production, commission of agents, transportation and other expenses. On the other hand the price at which the crops are sold may be lower than the cost of production if the cultivators are in urgent need of cash and are therefore compelled to sell their produce at a price which may not be high enough to cover even their cost of production. Higher margins which the farmers of large holding sizes are able to obtain, due to better bargaining strength and due to higher financial capacity, encourages farmers belonging to this group to offer more as marketed surplus. In contrast, lower level of margin for just the opposite reasons discourages them to offer less for sale. It is therefore pertinent that we specify a model, with the average level of margin for all the size holdings as an important explanatory variable. As a result the model takes the following form:

$$NMS = a + b\ Mrg + Ui \qquad \ldots(8)$$

Where Mrg = Margin, defined as the difference between

the sale of marketed surplus and total cost till the produce is brought to the market place.

The result of the estimated equation for the Valley as whole is as follow:

$$NMS = 496.178 + 3.487\ Mrg + Ui \qquad R^2 = .496\ F = 9.895$$
$$(3.975) \quad (92.84)$$

The results reveal that R^2 which is .496 is also significant Therefore 50 per cent of the relationship is explained by this function and the coefficient of the independent variable is not only statistically significant but it also explains the positive relationship between the net marketed surplus and the margin. Higher the margin higher also is the marketed surplus. In fact the elasticity of marketed surplus to margin is greater than unity, implying that profit represented by the extent of margin is one of the most crucial determinant of marketed surplus in the Valley.

Therefore once again, trying to analyse the result at a disaggregative level for the two categories of farmers and testing the models for the same reveal the following results:

Small Size holdings:

$$NMS = 317.870 + 1.838\ Mrg + Ui$$
$$(2.441) \quad (1.964)$$
$$R^2 = .349;\ F = 2.148$$

Large Size holdings:

$$NMS = 676.98 + 2.276\ Mrg + Ui$$
$$(.651) \quad (.254)$$
$$R^2 = .015;\ F = -.067$$

The results of the above equations indicate that the function cannot be accepted for the smaller holding size for the reasons discussed above. The function though slightly better for the small farmers however, does not appear to be too strong as an explanatory variable for marketed surplus. In other words, small and marginal farmers may often fail to get a higher margin due to their weak bargaining power. Consequently, to expect that they will determine the quantum of marketed surplus on the basis of their margin may be highly unrealistic. However, better prices due to extraneous factors may occasionally help them to enjoy a good margin.

Apart from the determinants of marketed surplus represented in the models above, some of the other important factors identified in the earlier chapter was the level of literacy of the farmers and the degree of their awareness regarding the market price and other related information. In an attempt to examine the exact quantitative relationship between these factors and marketed surplus the following models have also been tested:

$$NMS = a + b\ Lit + Ui \qquad \ldots(9)$$
$$NMS = a + b\ Awr + Ui \qquad \ldots(10)$$

Where

Lit = literacy rate of the farmers

Awr = awareness of the farmers about the market price of paddy

The estimated results of the function is as follows:

$$NMS = -203.517 + 12.639\ Lit + Ui$$
$$(-.255) \qquad (9.975)$$
$$R^2 = .087: F = .950$$

$$NMS = -312.12 + 17.34\ Awr + Ui$$
$$(-1.132) \quad (3.478)$$
$$R^2 = .548\ F = 12.10$$

From the results of the above models, it is revealed that literacy on the whole do not seem to have much impact on marketed surplus, which is a little surprising. However, the reason could be that literacy rate or the level of education is a socio-economic variable. As a result, though education is extremely important, yet its impact on market surplus may be indirect, the impact of which may be spread over a period of time. Therefore literacy rate for the cross section of the sample size at a particular point of time may not appear to be acceptable.

However, though literacy may not be acceptable as an explanatory variable, the awareness level of the farmers, which may be taken as a proxy for literacy level appear to be a crucial variable for our purpose. When farmers are aware of the price that is prevailing in the market, they are able to decide whether to offer their produce in the market or hold back their produce for a favorable time in the future when prices and consequently margins may also be high. Apart from this, direct impact of the awareness level may also have an indirect as well secondary effect. For instance, cultivators need to be aware not only about the price of the product but also sources of credit, farming techniques, information about the right place and persons to whom the surplus is to be sold. Consequently, we find from our estimated equation that more than fifty per cent of the relationship is explained by the level of awareness of the farmers. The coefficient of awareness is therefore satisfactory both on statistical as well as on theoretical grounds.

The other factors that are important in the determination of marketed surplus are the proportion of income of the farmers arising out of non agricultural sources and the proportion of agricultural income to total income. The reasons for the significance of these factors have already been discussed earlier. The models for our purpose with the proportion of agricultural and non agricultural income are of the following type:

$$NMS = a + b\ Nonagi + Ui \qquad \dots(11)$$

$$NMS = a + b\,Agi + Ui \qquad ...(12)$$

Where

nonagi = proportion of non agricultural income
Agi = proportion of agricultural income

The estimated equation reveal that the former model is unacceptable, because the results of the equation is as follows:

$$NMS = -18.996 + 23.106\ nonagi + Ui$$
$$(-.051) \quad (1.689) \qquad R^2 = .222;\ F = 2.852$$

Only 22 per cent of the relationship is explained by the function and the coefficient of the independent variable is insignificant and therefore the sign of the coefficient do not have any significance.

The estimated result of the second equation reveals the following results:

$$NMS = -463.72 + 34.097\ Agi + Ui$$
$$(-2.281) \quad (95.537)$$
$$R^2 = .754;\ F = 30.664$$

The above function is acceptable as R^2 is as high as 754 and the independent variable is not only statistically significant, but the positive sign of the coefficient implies, that higher the proportion of income from agriculture out of the total income of the farmers higher is also his incentive to offer more as marketed surplus. This may imply that higher income from agriculture may mean that cultivation is their main occupation and therefore they have the desire to raise marketed surplus, which may therefore enhance their total income. In contrast, if farmers can obtain their income from non agricultural sources their dependence on agricultural income is not high and they are therefore not very keen to increase their quantum of marketed surplus, since they are already well off.

It may therefore be evident from our analysis relating to the crucial determinants of marketed surplus in Barak Valley, that some of the variables such as total retention, production of paddy, level of awareness of the farmers, margins obtained by the sale of paddy and proportion of agricultural income to total income can be identified to be playing a pivotal role in determining the pattern of marketed surplus at a macro level.

We will therefore specify some more models which will take the above mentioned significant determinants as independent variables, the combined operation of which will be taken into account for the determination of marketed surplus along with their relative weigtage. The models used for the purpose will be as follows:

$$NMS = a + b\,Prod + c\,Reten + Ui \qquad \ldots(13)$$

$$NMS = a + b\,Prod + c\,Ret + d\,Mrg + Ui \qquad \ldots(14)$$

$$NMS = a + b\,Prod + c\,Ret + dMrg + e\,Awr + f\,Nagri + Ui \qquad \ldots(15)$$

$$NMS = a + b\,Prod + c\,Ret + d\,Mrg + e\,AWr + f\,Nagri + g\,Agri + Ui \qquad \ldots(16)$$

The estimated results of the models mentioned above are stated below:

$$NMS = -202.652 + .271\,Prod + .417\,Ret + Ui$$
$$(-1.008) \quad (1.685) \quad (.955)$$
$$R^2 = .791;\ F = 17.079$$

$$NMS = -177.349 + .335\,Prod - 2.66\,Ret + 2.017\,Mrg + Ui$$
$$(-1.226) \quad (2.849) \quad (-.076) \quad (93.009)$$
$$R^2 = .904,\ F = 25.181$$

$$NMS = 71.851 + .317\ Prod + 8.32\ Ret + 2.292\ Mrg - 2.441\ Awr$$
$$(-.202) \quad (2.33) \quad (.166) \quad (2.103) \quad (-.328)$$
$$R^2 = .906:\ F = 16.806$$

$$NMS = -127.313 + .305\ Prod + 7.508\ Ret + 2.238\ Mrg$$
$$(.312) \quad (2.055) \quad (.140) \quad (1.908)$$
$$-2.047\ Awr + 2.611\ Nargi + Ui$$
$$(-.256) \quad (.372)$$
$$R^2 = .908:\ F = 11.81$$

$$NMS = -761.677 + .142\ Prod + .159\ Ret - .149\ Mrg$$
$$(-2.527) \quad (1.431) \quad (.503) \quad (-.153)$$
$$-3.858\ Awr + 11.688\ Nagri + 28.432 Agri + Ui$$
$$(-.812) \quad (2.393) \quad (3.50)$$
$$R^2 - .973\ F = 30.354$$

Examination of the results of the estimated equations presented above clearly reveal that the explanatory power of the equations increase with the inclusion of the additional variables. The value of R^2 increases from .791 with production and retention as the only explanatory variables, to .904 with the inclusion of the percentage of margin as another variable. Addition of the extent of awareness as an additional variable increases R^2 to .906 and further to .928 with the addition of non agricultural income which is the highest at .973, when all the independent variables such as production, amount of retention, percentage of margin, level of awareness of the farmers and both income from agricultural as well as non agricultural sources are included in the function. This only goes to imply that all these factors in combination determine the marketed surplus of paddy in the Valley. However, examining the equations at greater depth, reveals that all the models cannot be accepted for our purpose, high degree of explanatory power of the variables notwithstanding. In the first of these equations, it is revealed that though production emerged as explanatory variable which may be accepted, yet with the addition of retention as another variable the sign of the coefficient of production has gone down relatively, and none of the two coefficients can be acceptable due to the insignificance of the value of the coefficients. The reason as to why retention cannot be acceptable for all the farmers at the macro level has already been discussed earlier. Inclusion of awareness of the farmers as an additional variable, though increases the explanatory power of the function, but the change in the size of the coefficient on awareness implies the presence of multi collinearity, which of course is not surprising in the case of the variables selected by us, which are highly correlated among themselves. Presence of multicollinearity and insignificant coefficient do not allow us to accept this function on statistical grounds.

In view of the non-significance of the coefficient of retention individually as an explanatory variable as well as in combination with other variables we have dropped this variable from the function and proceeded with the other independent variables in view of the reasons stated above. We have further added one more variable which is the proportion of non agricultural income. The result has been sudden increase in the explanatory power of the function to .928 from .906, yet the function cannot be accepted due to the insignificant values of the coefficient, with the exception of the coefficient of production. Consequently, we have decided to drop this function as well.

Lastly, we have tried another function, in which as before we have dropped retention as an explanatory variable, but incorporated the variables, such as production, margin, awareness, income from non agricultural sources. It is revealed that the value of R^2 is the highest in this case being as high as .973. This implies that almost the entire relationship of marketed surplus is explained by this function, in which the above mentioned variables have been incorporated. The results of the estimated equations reveal that though the explanatory power of the production coefficient has diminished slightly, nevertheless it retains its significance, because after all, though it may not be too important for the small and marginal farmers but it assumes its importance as far as the rich farmers are concerned. Coefficients of all the other variables are statistically significant and theoretically acceptable. Though the sign of the coefficient on awareness has changed from being positive when taken as an independent variable to negative when combined with other variables, we accept it in the new form, because awareness can play both a positive as well as a negative role. This is because when awareness of unfavorable market price or market condition is available to the farmers marketed surplus may go down with higher degree of awareness. At other times, with higher degree of awareness regarding the favourable market condition marketed surplus may actually rise. Consequently, awareness in combination with other independent variables has throughout retained its negative sign. We therefore do not discard it, but view it in a different light.

5.3 Conclusion

Taking a holistic view therefore, we accept that model which incorporates the variables such as production, margin, level of awareness and income from both agricultural as well as non agricultural sources as the crucial determinants of marketed surplus in Barak Valley, since almost the entire variation is explained by this function. However, a word of caution, needs to be mentioned here that break up of the study at micro level for the small and marginal farmers on the one hand and big farmers on the other has certainly highlighted the fact that same set of factors may not assume a similar degree of importance in expalaining marketed surplus. However, the above mentioned factors on the whole can be accepted to govern the behaviourial pattern of marketed surplus in the Valley.

References

Acharya, S.S. (2004) *"State of the Indian Farmers"*, Ministry of Agriculture Volume, 17, GoI, New Delhi.

Agarwal A.L. (1970): "Marketable Agricultural Surplus in Relation to Size of Land Holdings—A Case Study (UP)," *Agricultural Situation in India,* Volume 25.

Dandekar, V. M (1964) "Prices, Production and Marketable Surplus of Foodgrains", *Indian Journal of Agricultural Economics,* Volume 19.

Goswami, P.C. and Saikia, P.D. (1968): "Disposals of Paddy by Surplus Growers—A Study of Assam", *Economic and Political Weekly,* Volume 3.

Hati, Ashok (1976): "Non Linear Marketable Surplus Functions", *Economic and Political Weekly,* Volume XI, No. 27.

Jakahade, V.M. and Mazumdar, N.A. (1964): "Response of Agricultural Producers to Prices—The Case of Jute and Rice in India", *Indian Journal of Agricultural Economics,* Volume 19.

Kahloon, A.S. and Dwivedi, H.N. (1963): "Interrelationship between Production and Marketable Surplus" *Assam, Economic Review.*

Kahloon, A.S. and Vasistha V.V. (1968): "A Study of Factors Governing the Flow of Marketable Surplus of Major Crops in Ludhiana District", *Agricultural Situation in India,* Volume 23.

Krishna, Raj (1965): "The Marketable Surplus Function for a Subsistence Crop.—An Analysis with Indian Data", *The Economic Weekly,* Volume 17.

Krishnan, T.N. (1965): "The Marketable Surplus of Foodgrains: Is it inversely related to Prices?", *The Economic Weekly,* Vol. 17.

Mathur, P.N. and Ezekiel, H. (1961): "Marketable Surplus of Food and Price Fluctuations in a Developing Economy", *Kyklos,* Volume 14.

Muthaiah, C. (1964): "Marketed Surplus of Foodgrains by Size of Holdings and Income", *Agricultural Situation in India,* Vol. 19.

Narain, D. (1961): "Distribution of Marketed Surplus of Agricultural Produce by Size Levels of Holdings in India, 1950-51", Institute of Economic Growth, Asia Publishing House, Bombay.

Patnaik, Utsa (1975): "Contribution to Output and Marketable Surplus of Agricultural Products by Cultivationg Groups in India, 1960-61", *Economic and Political Weekly,* Vol. 10, No. 52

Prasad, J. (1989): *"Marketable Surplus and Market Performance"* Mittal Publications Delhi.

Sharma, P.P. (1968): "Subsistence Crops—Consumption and Marketable Surplus", *Economic and Political Weekly,* Vol. 3.

Sharma, P.S. (1972): "Estimation of "Marketable Surplus of Foodgrains by Size Class of Holdings: Some Preliminary Results", *Agricultural Situation in India,* Volume 19.

Sengupta, K. (1998): "Behaviourial Pattern of Marketable Surplus in Barak Valley of South Assam", *Agricultural Situation in India,* GoI, New Delhi. Vol. ?.

Upendra, M. (1990): *"Marketable and Marketed Surplus in Agriculture"*, Mittal Publications, New Delhi.

6

Conclusions and Main Findings

In the present section we will make a brief statement of the main findings of the present study, which will thereby enable us to capture the essence of the present work. The crucial findings would be helpful for the policy makers as well as the researchers in this area of study in the future. One important finding of the study is that no single factor alone can govern the generation of marketed surplus in the Valley. In fact, not only a number of factors are in operation simultaneously, but a different set of factors operate with various degrees of strength at different times. Yet another important aspect which emerges out of this study is that the factors that play a significant role in the determination of marketed surplus for small size holdings often do not have similar role in the determination of marketed surplus for large size holdings, in whose case other factors assume greater importance in determining such surpluses.

Taking an overall perspective, the study reveals that marketed surplus generated in the Valley amounts to 43.91 per cent of the total production. Unlike the "U" pattern of behaviour of marketed surplus as in some studies the behaviourial pattern of marketed surplus in this Valley increases in direct proportion to holding size as maintained by Patnaik and others in their study. Though the proportion of marketed surplus to total output for the larger size holdings is comparable to marketable surplus generated in other states, the marketable surplus of smaller size holdings is much below the all India average. This finding reveals the extreme poverty of the small and marginal farmers and the fact that agriculture is still carried on mostly on a subsistence basis and not commercial basis in this Valley. The study further reveals that small farmers have to retain a larger share of their production for various types of financial obligations and payments are made by them mostly in kind in terms of paddy, reducing to that extent the ability to generate marketable surplus.

It is also revealed that marketable surplus for all size holdings exceed marketed surplus. This is an experience which is not in conformity with other parts of the country where marketed and marketable surplus tends to be equal for small farmers due to distress sale and the inability of the farmers to hold back stocks, either due to financial compulsion or lack of space. Though the difference between marketable and marketed surplus is insignificant in case of small size holdings, it clearly shows a rising tendency along with a rise in holding size. Presence of distress sale among small farmers is clearly identified as an important explanatory factor responsible for the small difference between marketable and marketed surplus. The wider gap between the two among large farmers indicates their relative prosperity. It not only shows that they have the power to hold back the stock and are also not in need of immediate cash on an urgent basis. Such farmers also have adequate storage facilities due to which a considerable extent of gap between marketable and marketed surplus is observed. Distress sale decrease directly with the increase in size of land holdings.

Poverty of the small and marginal farmers in the Valley is further evident from the fact that such farmers repurchase the highest quantity of paddy from the market and other farmers. However, at the same time, it also needs to be mentioned that there is no record of negative marketed surplus among the farmers of this Valley when repurchase from the market exceed the total quantum of sale. In this respect the position of the farmers of this Valley is superior to that of farmers in other parts of the country.

The study further reveals that retention is an important determinant of marketed surplus, though the impact of retention is not uniform for all size holdings. Retention for the purpose of consumption accounts for 30.67 per cent of the current output in the Valley.The proportion of such retention however, decreases in direct proportion to holding size. In contrast, retention for the purpose of sale in the future increases in direct proportion to holding size. On the whole about 14 per cent of the produce is held back from the market for the purpose of future sale. An interesting feature that emerges out of the present study is that even the small farmers retain a very small quantity for the purpose of future sale, a feature which is not evident in other parts of the country.

Another feature which emerges from the study is that the deviation of price per quintal from the average price at which farmers sell their produce in the market is the highest for the small farmers and the deviation gradually goes on declining along with increase in holding size. This indicates the poor bargaining position of the farmers in the Valley. Lower remunerative prices acts as a serious deterrent to the generation of marketed surplus as well as increase in production. Prices have both a forward as well as backward linkage with marketed surplus. Just as lower prices reduce marketed surplus lower marketed surplus does not allow price to be an indicator of the correct market signal. Prices therefore emerge as an important determinant of marketed surplus. Apart from prices the extent of margin, that is the difference between price at which paddy is sold and the cost of production, emerges as another important determinant of marketed surplus. Small and marginal farmers often sell the produce at a negative price, which is a price much below the cost of production. In contrast, farmers of large holdings sell the produce with a positive margin which goes on increasing with holding size. The study also reveals that the extent of margin earned and the volume of marketed surplus generated are directly correlated, implying that margin is an important determinant of marketed surplus in this Valley.

It is interesting to note from the findings that small and marginal farmers sell a greater proportion of their produce immediately in the post harvest season, whereas farmers belonging to large size holdings sell a smaller proportion during this period, but larger proportion during the lean season. Such findings however are on expected lines and are similar to findings in other parts of the country. It is also revealed that farmers belonging to large size holdings sell the maximum proportion of their produce through middlemen and only a very small proportion sell directly in the market. In contrast, small farmers' dependence on the middlemen is totally insignificant, since all farmers belonging to this group sell the produce directly in the market without going through the middlemen.

The level of awareness relating to the market price of paddy appears to be an important determinant factor of marketed surplus. It is revealed that small and marginal farmers are often not aware of the ruling market price and therefore tend to sell at a rate when prices are the lowest. This is an experience which is not evident among farmers of large size holdings.

An indepth examination of the various components of retention reveal that though retention is important, for all size holdings, yet different component of retention assume different extent of importance for different size holdings. The study reveals that retention for consumption play a greater role while for others, retention for the purpose of wage payments seeds or for future sales assume a greater importance. An interesting finding of the study is that though consumption as a component of retention emerges to be an important determinant factor yet for the small and marginal farmers consumption does not appear to be an important determinant factor. This is not in conformity with any study conducted on such lines earlier. The reasons for such behaviour in this Valley are not far to seek. Most of these farmers in this Valley are very poor and conduct agriculture on subsistence basis. Due to the urgent need for cash, they are compelled to sell whatever they have produced immediately in the post harvest season. As a result their capacity for retention for the purpose of consumption is low and hence consumption is not an important determinant factor of marketed surplus for them. They indulge in repurchase from the market for their own consumption at a later period often at a higher price. However, retention for consumption for farmers of large size holdings emerges to be an important determinant factor. Such farmers have holding capacity and are also not in need of immediate cash and thus are in a position to govern the pattern of marketed surplus through their decision to retain the requisite portion of the output.

When we take the behaviourial pattern of marketable surplus for the Valley as a whole, retention for the purpose of future sale does not occupy a significant position signifying the non-commercial nature of production in the Valley.

Production in all places assume a significant role in the determination of marketed surplus. In Barak Valley too 40 per cent of the change in net marketed surplus is determined by the quantum of marketed surplus. However a deeper analysis of the study reveals that production does not explain the behaviourial pattern of marketed surplus among small and marginal farmers. Increased production results in higher level of self consumption rather than higher volume of sales. This is a typical situation where agricultural production is carried on a subsistence basis. For such farmers price incentives play a greater role rather than production incentives. In contrast, production plays a dominant role in determining marketed surplus among farmers of large size holdings because they not only conduct agriculture on a commercial basis, but their marginal propensity to consume too is low. Consequently, higher level of production does not result in higher level of consumption but in higher sale. In fact, that is the reason why production explains 87 per cent of the variation in NMS among farmers of this group.

Price as a determinant of marketed surplus too plays different role for different category of farmers. Price according to this study emerges to be an important determinant among small farmers, though the same is not true among farmers of large size holdings. Small and marginal farmers even at the cost of lower self-consumption are willing to offer a larger quantum for sale provided they are certain of obtaining a higher price. Farmers belonging to large size holdings on the other hand though appreciate higher prices in marketing practices are influenced more by the level of production in their decision on the quantum of sale.

A significant finding of the study on the whole is that marketed surplus is affected by a number of factors, yet all factors do not occupy the same degree of significance for different groups of farmers.

Bibliography

Acharya, S. (2004): *"State of the Indian Farmer"* Ministry of Agriculture, Volume 17, GoI, New Delhi.

Agarwal, A.L. (1970): "Marketed Agricultural Surpluses in Relation to Size of Land Holdings—A Case Study (UP)", *Agricultural Situation of India*, GoI, Vol. 25.

Agarwal, N.L. (1986): *"Agricultural Prices and Marketing in India"* Mittal Publication, New Delhi.

Bardhan, Pranab and Kalpana, Bardhan (1968): "The Problem of Marketed Surplus of Cereals", *Economic and Political Weekly*, Volume IV, No 26, 29.

Basic Statistics of North Eastern Region: Various Issues, North Eastern Council, Shillong.

Bhargava, P.N. and V.S. Rastogi (1972): "Study of Marketable Surplus of Paddy in Burdwan District" *Indian Journal of Agricultural Economics,* Vol. 27.

Chakraborty, R.M. (1986): "Marketable Surplus of Foodgrains in Developing Economy", *Arthaniti,* Vol. II.

Dandekar, V.M. (1964): "Prices, Production and Marketed Surplus of Foodgrains", *Indian Journal of Agricultural Economics*, Vol. 19.

Dubey, V. (1963): "The Marketed Agricultural Surplus and Economic Growth in Underdeveloped Countries", *Economic Journal*, Vol. 73.

Economic Survey of Assam: Various Issues, Directorate of Economics and Statistics, Government of Assam, Guwahati.

Gangwar, A.C. and Goel, R.C. (1980): "Impact of Green Revolution of Marketing Costs and Margins of Rice in Haryana", *Agricultural Marketing,* Vol. 22.

Goswami, P.C. and P.D. Saikia (1968): "Disposables of Paddy by Surplus Growers—A Study of Assam", *Economic and Political Weekly,* Vol. 3.

Gupta, G.S. (1980): "Agricultural Price Policies and Farm Incomes", *Economic and Political Weekly,* Vol. XV.

Hati, Ashok (1976): "Non Linear Marketable Surplus Functions" *Economic and Political Weekly,* Vol. XI, No. 27

Jakhade, V.M. and N.A. Mazumdar, (1964): "Response of agricultural Producers to Prices—The Case of Jute and Rice in India", *Indian Journal of Agricultural Economics,* Vol. 19.

Kahlan, A.S. and Reed, C.E. (1961): "Problems of Marketable Surplus in Indian Agriculture", *Indian Journal of Agricultural Economics,* Vol. 16.

Kahlan, A.S. and V.V. Vashista (1968): "A Study of Factors Governing the Flow of Marketable Surplus of Major Crops in Ludhiana District", *Agricultural Situation in India,* Vol. 23.

Kaul, J.L. and D.S. Sindhu (1971): "Acreage Response to Prices for major Crops in Punjab—An Econometric Study", *Indian Journal of Agricultural Economics,* Vol. 26.

Krishna, Raj (1965): "The Marketable Surplus Function for a Subsistence Crop", *Indian Journal of Agricultural Economics,* Vol. 17.

Krishna, Raj (1965): "The Marketable Surplus Function for a Subsistence Crop—An Analysis with Indian Data", *The Economic Weekly,* Vol. 17.

Krishnan, T.N. (1965): "The Marketed Surplus of Foodgrains: Is it inversely related to Prices?", *The Economic Weekly,* Vol. 17.

Laksmanan, P.P. (1967): "Transport of Paddy from the Farms to the Markets in India", *Agricultural Situation in India,* Volume XXII, No 3.

Mandal, G.C. (1967): "Agricultural Surplus, Labour Surplus and Economic Development—A Theoretical Approach", *Indian Journal of Agricultural Economics,* Vol. 23.

Mandal, G.C. and H.G. Ghosh (1968): "A Study of Marketed Surplus of Paddy at the Farm Level in Four East Indian Villages", *Indian Journal of Agricultural Economics,* Vol. 23.

Mathan, P.K. (1970): "Role of Marketable Food Surplus in Economic Development" Asian Economic Review Vol. 12.

Mathur, P.N. (1959): "Time Pattern and Quantum of Purchase and Sale of Jowar by Peasants of Vidharbha (Bombay State)" *Artha Vijana*, Vol. I.

Mathur, P.N. and H. Ezekiel (1961): "Marketable Surplus Function of Food and Price Fluctuations in a Developing Economy", *Kyklos*, Vol. 14.

Minacha, A.G. (1967): "Marketable Surplus of Agriculture and Economic Growth in India" in Jain, S.C. (Ed) *Problems of Agricultural Development in India*, Kitab Mahal, Allahabad.

Muthaiah, C. (1964): "Marketable Surplus of Foodgrains by Size Holdings and Income", *Agricultural Situation in India*, Vol. 19.

——————— (1980): "Marketable Surplus, Market Dependence and Economic Development", *Social Scientist*, Vol. 7.

Mazumdar, A.P., Archarjee P. and J. Bhattacherjee (1998): *"Statistical Profile of Barak Valley"*, NECAS, Silchar, Assam.

Naqvi, S. (1961): "Problems of Marketable Surplus in Indian Agriculture", *Indian Journal of Agricultural Economics*, Vol. 16.

Narain, D. (1961): *"Distribution of Marketed Surplus of Agricultural Produce by Size Level of Holdings in India 1950-51"*, Asia Publishing House, Bombay.

Natarajan, B. (1961): "Problems of Marketable Surplus in Indian Agriculture", *Indian Journal of Agricultural Economics*, Vol. 16.

Nichollas, W.H. (1963) : "An Agricultural Surplus as a Factor in Economic Dev." Journal of Political Economy Vol. 7.

Parthasarathy, P.B. and M. Kamalakar (1975): "Marketable and Marketed Surplus in Paddy and Groundnuts of Small Farms" *Indian Journal of Agricultural Economics*, Vol. 30. No. 3

Parashar, P.K. (1969): "Marketing Channels in Developing Economies", *Agricultural Situation in India*, Vol. 23, No 12.

Parashar, and Subha B.V. (1984): "Production and Marketed Surplus of Rice in the Deltas of the South", *Agricultural Situation in India*, Vol. 21.

Patnaik, Utsa (1975): "Contribution to the Output and Marketable Surplus of Agricultural Products by Cultivating Groups in India, 1960-61", *Economic and Political Weekly*, Vol. 10. No.. 52.

Poduval, R.N. (1958): "Economic Development and Marketed Surplus in Agriculture", *Agricultural Situation in India*, Vol. 13.

Prasad, J. (1989): *"Marketable Surplus and Market Performance"*, Mittal Publication, New Delhi.

Prasad, K.N. (1999): "*Agricultural Marketing: Problems and Prospects*" in *Encyclopaedia of Agricultural Marketing* ed. J. Prasad, Mittal Publication, New Delhi.

Prasad, J. (1999): "Agricultural Marketing System in Bihar: Emerging Trends and Perspectives" in *Encyclopaedia of Agricultural Marketing* ed J. Prasad, Mittal Publication, New Delhi.

Prasad, Pradhan H. (1999): "Agricultural Marketing in India: Some Burning Issues" in *Encyclopaedia of Agricultural Marketing* ed. J. Prasad, Mittal Publication New Delhi.

Prasad, Sivarama (1985): "*Agricultural Marketing in India*" Mittal Publications, New Delhi.

Prasad, A and J.Prasad (1994): "*Development Planning for Agriculture*", Mittal Publication, New Delhi.

Rajagopal, (1999): "Development of Agricultural Marketing in India" in *Encyclopaedia of Agricultural Marketing* ed J. Prasad, Mittal Publication, New Delhi.

Ram, S. (1976): "Note on the Marketable Surplus in Wheat" *Indian Journal of Agricultural Economics*, Vol. 10.

Ramachandran, V. and T.P. Gopalaswamy (1975): "Impact of Area Under HYV on Marketable Surplus of Paddy in West Godavari District" *Agricultural Situation in India*, Vol. 30.

Rao, C.H. Hanumantha (1977): "The Marketable Surplus Function for a Subsistence Crop", Comments *Economic Weekly*, Vol. 17.

Rao, P.V.G.K. (1965): "Marketable Surplus and Agricultural Production—A Case Study of a Village in UP", *Agricultural Situation in India*, Vol. 20.

Rao, V. Srinivasa (1961): "A Study of Marketed Surplus of Foodgrains with Special Reference to Selected Villages in South India", *Indian Journal of Agricultural Economics*, Vol. 16.

Reddy, M.J.M. (1987): "Marketable Surplus in Paddy: A Regression Analysis", *Agricultural Situation in India*. Vol. ?

Rudra, A. (1973): "Marketing Behaviour of Big, Medium and Small Farmers", *Economic and Political Weekly*, Vol. II, No. 27.

Saran, Ram (1961): "Problems of Marketable Surplus of Foodgrains in India", *Indian Journal of Agricultural Economics*, Vol. 16.

Statistical Handbook of Assam: Various Issues Directorate of Economics and Statistics Government of Assam.

Saxena, B.S. (1961): "Problems of Marketable Surplus in Indian Agriculture", *Indian Journal of Agricultural Economics*, Vol. 16.

Sengupta K. (1992): "Genesis of Inflation in India: A Diagnostic Analysis" Finance India, Vol. XI, New Delhi.

Sharma, P.P. (1969): "Marketable Surplus in Subsistence Crops: A Case Study of a District Village in Rajasthan" *Economic and Political Weekly,* Vol. 4.

Sharma, P.P. (1968): "Subsistence Crops—Consumption and Marketable Surplus" *Economic and Political Weekly,* Vol. 3.

Sharma, P.S. (1972): "Estimation of Marketable Surplus of Foodgrains by Size Class of Holdings Some Preliminary Results" *Agricultural Situation in India,* Vol. 19.

Shastri, C.P. (1963): "Inter relationship between Production, Prices and Marketable Surplus in Bihar" *Agricultural Situation in India,* Vol. 18.

Shukla, G.S. (1999): "Planning for the Developments of Rural Markets" in *Encyclopedia of Agricultural Marketing* ed. J. Prasad, Mittal Publication, New Delhi.

Sinha, S.N. (1962): "Marketable Surplus in Agriculture in Underdeveloped Countries", *Indian Economic Review,* Vol. 17.

Singh, S.K. (1999): "Agricultural Marketing in India: Issues and Options" in *Encyclopedia of Agricultural Marketing* ed. J. Prasad, Mittal Publication, New Delhi.

Srinivasan, M. (1961): "Problems of Agricultural Marketing in Indian Agriculture" *Indian Journal of Agricultural Economics,* Vol. 16.

Sengupta, K. (1998); "Behaviourial Pattern of Marketable Surplus in Barak Valley of South Assam" *Agricultural Situation in India.* Government of India, New Delhi.

Thamavajakshi, R. (1971): "Prices, Production and Marketed Surplus of Foograins in the Indian Economy 1951-52/1965-66" *Agricultural Situation in India,* Vol. 25.

Upendra, M. (1990)"*Marketable and Marketed Surplus in Agriculture*", Mittal Publications, New Delhi.

Vyas, V.S. and H.H. Maharaja (1966): "Factors Affecting Marketable Surplus and Marketed Supplies—A Case Study of the Region in Gujarat and Rajasthan", *Artha Vikas,* Vol. 2. No. 1.

Index